TURKEY HUNTING
A One Man Game

TURKEY HUNTING
A One Man Game

by Ken Morgan

Sketches by Billy DeMoss

Photography by William Yarbrough, Dave Moreland,
Butch Trahan and Ken Morgan

Copyright © 1987
by Ken Morgan
Reprinted March 2014
by Morgan's Turkey Callers, LLC
Sally Stuart Morgan

Available from:
Morgan's Turkey Callers, LLC
Baton Rouge, LA 70808
www.turkeycallers.com
www.wildturkeys.com

Printing by
Vivid Ink Printing
Baton Rouge, LA 70809

*Dedicated to the memory of
Lu Howell, our good friend and
master turkey hunter.*

Table of Contents

Foreword   ix

Preface   xiii

PART ONE: Selected Hunting Experiences and Miscellaneous Facts

    1 Brother Van's Poor Old Gobbler   5
    2 Gobbler on a Ledge   15
    3 Buster and Dad   25
    4 A Mid Day Gobbler to Remember   31
    5 The Green Dragon Gobbler   41
    6 The Circuit Rider   51
    7 The Mystery of Little Beaver Creek   65
    8 A Very Weird Hunt   75

PART TWO: Calling, Hunting, and Peculiarities of the Wild Turkey

    9 The Art of Calling Springtime Gobblers   83
    10 Stealth   101
    11 Master of Evasion and Escape   117
    12 The Preferred Male   129

PART THREE: Management of Turkeys and People

    13 Put Something Back   141
    14 Please Be Careful   173
    15 The Turkey Hunting Fraternity   181

"Lu" Howell   191

Foreword

The author's reputation had preceded him. "If Ken Morgan says a rooster can pull a train, hitch him up and tell him, 'shoo'". So said Glen Whetstone, my original turkey mentor, and possibly the most patient and efficient of all turkey hunters with whom I have been associated.

I met Kenny and killed my first gobbler on the same afternoon, April 12, 1975. I lost my "Morgan Call" when I jumped up to run to my turkey at the shot. I looked and looked, but could not find the caller. After photographing and admiring that fine bird for what is always an insufficient period of time, I jumped into the truck and visited all the sporting goods stores within a forty mile radius trying desperately to find another caller. Luckily, my search was fruitless. My only recourse was to drive to Jackson and find the manufacturer. I asked around for directions and finally located his house. No one was home. I waited two hours until the master finally arrived. I left two hours later with a new call, a new friend, and a new insight into the most fascinating of sports.

I have been favored to spend a minimum of two hundred nights with Ken, his family, and friends. I have sat down to the finest home cooking anywhere prepared by Ken's beautiful wife, Linda, who amazes me with her patience and understanding of the turkey hunting disease afflicting her husband and seemingly all of his close companions. I have watched their daughter, Vicki, grow from a mere tot into a beautiful eighteen year old LSU Coed. I have shared the Morgans' sorrows, joys, sicknesses and their health. The Morgans are family to me.

The wild turkey is the focus of this relationship, and no one understands this creature as Ken does. Many mornings have I driven over one hundred miles to greet the morning dawn only to find Ken clothed only in his underwear and socks standing sleepily on the porch with the welcoming announcement, "they ain't gonna gobble this morning". Whereupon he would go back to bed. I can't remember a single turkey gobbling on the mornings of these proclamations and on some of the seemingly most beautiful mornings you can imagine. In fact, one often finds Ken in a laid back posture whereupon he will direct a total stranger into the lap of the finest gobbler in the Felicianas. He enjoys predicting the death of a wary old gobbler by having his constituents follow his instructions, having already observed the particular gobbler at close range and having decided that he did not want to kill the bird.

Other times will find Ken with a strange look in his eye and in close company with his callers and shotgun. I feel sorry for the turkeys on those mornings, for some poor chosen bird is most surely going to die. I have found the quickest way to see a dead gobbler is to announce to Ken that a certain area has no turkey gobblers. Nothing so sets his resolve. I and others have made the fatal mistake of commenting, "No gobblers on the place," only to have him in there the next morning and create the grandaddy of them all. I now say "I didn't see any sign" or "I didn't hear any". You'll not catch me saying, "there ain't no turkeys there".

Kenny appears to know every gobbler within the ten mile square area which is his principal baliwick. Late in the season, when most hunters have quit because of a lack of gobblers, Ken can sit and pinpoint twenty adults and forty untouchable jakes. Of the twenty adults, he will most likely have decided that sixteen shall be spared to grow a little older and wiser. I originally questioned Ken's management techniques thinking that a bird in the hand . . . , however eleven years of observation has convinced me of the soundness of his management decisions.

Kenny is at his best when predicting where a particular boss gobbler will walk. Many times has he directed me to a certain spot from which to call. One hunt in particular stands out in my memory.

"Walk south three ridges down the pipeline and sit beside the big beech tree on your right about twenty yards down the ridge road. You may have to stay until noon, but he's coming."

So started one of the most boring, yet maybe the most memorable turkey hunt of my fourteen year career. The hunt actually began the afternoon before when Butch Trahan and I rode together to a spot along big Thompson Creek that is composed of as fine a spring turkey range as there is in Louisiana. The area consists of deep hardwood hollows interspersed among about twenty pastures. Butch was to peruse the south end of the property, while I did the same to the north.

I was much greener in those days concerning the ways of the wild turkey, but I had learned that the only way to pursue these great birds is all by your lonesome. I had developed the bad, as well as dangerous habit of always keeping my gun loaded in the truck. This was done for two reasons. First, I didn't want to take the chance of forgetting to load my gun until I was within calling distance of a gobbler on the roost. I did have enough sense to know that the sound of metal signaled danger to a turkey. And one never knew when a hated canine might present a shot along some woods road. Despite a lack of concern for my own safety, I did have enough consideration for Butch to unload my shotgun at the car as we met following our unsuccessful hunt that evening. My anticipation factor was at its normal high level that night as I finally fell into a fitful slumber.

I consulted Kenny the next morning upon arising. He said that the huge gobbler was hanging out on the third ridge from the creek on the pipeline. He said that the turkey came out each morning on that ridge, but that he was quite irregular about the time he chose to show himself. "Don't leave before noon", he cautioned.

The pipeline runs north and south with beautiful beech ridges interspersed with other hardwoods running southwest to the creek. Across the creek lies another of those turkey springtime paradises, an intermixture of both large and small pastures broken by hardwood hollows. It was as fine a place to encounter a trophy gobbler as one could hope for. I say was, because now the pipeline is owned by a communal group I refer to as "the noise-makers". These people bought twenty acres in the middle of paradise and brought about ten housetrailers, several dogs, hogs, ponys, cows and a tame gobbler with them. The noise generated by these people is simply deafening. I still hunt along the area. There is something about the sound of young kids getting the hell beat out of them that brings back a part of my own childhood. There is also the need to constantly police the area. There is always a fine close-mouthed gobbler or two hanging around a ridge or so away from the confusion. And there are still the memories of the place it used to be. This particular hunt sticks out above all others because of the lessons taught that morning.

It was the kind of April morning that I would trade at least three of for one ideal clear frosty morning of mid to late March. The air was heavy enough to cut with a knife. It was hot and humid and foggy. I really didn't expect to hear a thing. My expectations were not disappointed; I was.

The first sound I heard was the song of Chuck Will's Widow as the night all too slowly turned to a gray dreary morning. A Yellow-breasted Chat began taunting me as if he knew that his song signals the end of the gobbling season. I waited patiently for the gobble that never came and after about an hour I constructed a blind at the base of Kenny's beech tree.

Left to my own designs, I began a favorite blind routine of alternately calling every fifteen and thirty minutes. The woods were silent as a tomb and they remained so. I would lightly yelp on one or two series and then cackle loudly on another. Sitting in that one spot was the most difficult hunting maneuver I had ever attempted. Remember, there was a fantastic springtime perusing territory lying just a half mile south of my position. I stood my ground.

At eleven fifteen, I heard the telltale crunch, crunch, manlike steps made only by two creatures in our part of the country. "Crunch, crunch, crunch", the sound became louder below the crest of the ridge. I raised my gun and sighted down the barrel.

The finest gobbler I had yet seen stepped in the road at eleven steps down my gun barrel. I released the safety and began a slow squeeze of the trigger.

"CLICK".

The giant gobbler was immediately airborne. My mistakes were immediately and indelibly burned into my consciousness. I now load and unload my gun at the truck. I have learned to silently check my shotgun at thirty minute intervals even when there was a shell in the chamber thirty minutes ago when I last looked. And I sit by that tree, or any other tree Ken Morgan tells me to sit by.

The reader is about to embark on a fantastic literary journey with the most amazing outdoorsman I have had the pleasure to know. Ken is going to unveil many of his secrets, secrets which have made him the premier turkey man of his era. Some of his techniques and secrets will be obvious to the reader, while others must be gleaned from the lines by careful dissection of his words. Hold on to your hat, Ken Morgan just hitched a rooster, no, a gobbler to your train.

BY WILLIAM YARBROUGH

Preface

Maybe there are some outdoor experiences which compare favorably with spring time turkey hunting, but I do not know about them. Perhaps there are more impressive sounds in nature than the vain and demanding call of an aggressive wild gobbler, but I have not heard them. Then too, there may be animals more wary and suspicious than a fully mature wild tom, but I have never seen them. At least more pleasant weather may be enjoyed at times other than the crisp mornings of early spring, but I have yet to experience the sensation. For the life of me, I can't recall anything which tickles my senses more than the thrills of turkey hunting. I have found many things to truly entertain me over the past forty years, but turkey hunting is far and away the most important vice which I have so far discovered.

All birds, not just the wild turkey, have held a particular appeal for me since I was introduced to "bird watching" by the late George Lowery, Ph.D., of the Louisiana State University Museum of Natural Science. Dr. Lowery was long my hero beginning at my chance meeting with him when I was very young, and continuing through my college days where I studied both ornithology and mammalogy under his tuteledge. "Doc" was known world wide for his life's work of studying and collecting bird specimens from everywhere on this planet. The impressions and training left upon me by the great mentor have contributed greatly to my interest in wild things, and in particular to my intense desire to discover the secrets of the great wild turkey which inhabits the fields and forests around my home.

I wish to write a book here which will deal primarily with the matters concerning the killing of mature wild gobblers in the spring. I will lay out some scientific facts and there will be a sprinkling of small doses of modern day management techniques. The main course, however, will remain an exercise on how to get the drop on the wily wild gobbler.

I was not prompted to write this book because of a shortage in the literature concerning the subject. There are volumes and volumes of writings dealing with this fine game bird and there is no end to the information we might assemble on *Meleagris gallopavo sylvestris*, the eastern wild turkey.

Admittedly, some of the information found within this mountain of literature is compatible in content with my own ideas, thoughts, and experiences with the wild turkey. This material is not my own though, and I would like very much to spell out some things about the wild turkey which were left completely out of books written before I decided to summarize for readers my thirty years of observations.

Assuming the wild turkey has similar traits in all parts of its range, my experiences may be valuable to those of you who want wild turkeys to prosper so that we may continue hunting them. I will try to relate some knowledge to the reader by recounting some of my own hunting triumphs and failures. (Some of our failures are far more instructive than are our triumphs.)

Hopefully, I can gain some insight by writing this book, and you can gather some information which will help you enjoy our great sport to the fullest. Read carefully, as I respect your own perceptive talents—since you are a turkey hunter.

Since turkey hunting is intended to be for our entertainment, maybe you can be a little amused also. The birds have amused me quite thoroughly.

Let me advise you that this book will certainly be far from complete. My opinions, hopefully, will be taken lightly to the heart and strongly to the head.

Lastly, please approach the reading and the game of turkey hunting itself with the idea that you will be hunting the birds alone. While it is extremely important to have close friends whose ear you can bend with wild tales of benign adventure, a solitary hunter alone in the woods gets the maximum amount of relaxation and pleasure from this One Man Game of ours.

TURKEY HUNTING
A One Man Game

PART ONE

Selected Hunting Experiences and Miscellaneous Facts

"Those little habits of theirs make them hard to kill"

1 Brother Van's Poor Old Gobbler

Since my last encounter with a boss gobbler is freshest on my mind, let me begin by telling you the story of how this fine old patriarch of the deep woods wound up in our freezer.

My brother Van and a group of fellows in a hunting club had pursued this particular turkey all through the 1985 season and into the final week of the season just past. They never fired a shot, but managed to run the gobbler all over several square miles of the prettiest turkey woods you ever saw. Strangely, the turkey never quit gobbling. Van said the only reason the bird gobbled was to draw a response from those folks calling him so the old boy would be able to get an accurate fix on the exact location of all the hunters who were after him. He claimed the turkey was playing a game with the hunters by gobbling violently at any caller.

Brother Van made the mistake of commenting that I could not come close to calling in this smart old cookie, that the bird would make a fool out of me too. Now, I'll be the first to admit that many gobblers have made a fool out of me, but I'll gladly take up the challenge of any stubborn and hunter-wise gobbler. I'm like most hunters; if the tom will gobble, I'll stay after him. It's fun to fool with a gobbling turkey whether you can get him or not.

Everybody in our little turkey hunting fraternity expected me to take up the chase. Van had kind of put me on the spot. I don't know who put their money on me and I don't know who put their money on the gobbler. After hearing about where the turkey was and how the gobbler was acting, they should have put their money on me. The gobbler's baliwick was in a locale where I have killed no fewer than twenty longbearded toms over the years. He was a gobbling fool, made to order for me.

The gobbler was located in one of my favorite places on earth; we call the area "the wilderness". The wilderness is roughly a sixteen square mile block of woods completely and one hundred percent owned by private landowners. Most of these landowners are very conservative with their timber cutting activities. This kind of timber management quite naturally lends itself to producing quality turkey woods.

Within these vast woodlands, there are no fewer than fifty little spring fed branches and creeks. All the spring branch heads have gone through a woodland plant succession; the timber species at the branch heads are mainly beech and magnolia. This had created fifty loafing and roosting places highly desirable to turkey flocks. Of course, many of the ridges are mixed pine-hardwood and a few ridges are almost pure oak. There are some pure pine ridges too, but almost all of the creek bottoms have plenty of quality hardwood stands. It is not only a place which is good for turkeys, it is also a good place to be on a spring morning.

There had been an outbreak of Southern Pine Beetles in the area where Van's turkey was located, and some eighty acres of pine had to be cut. This created an area highly attractive to nesting turkey hens with the low lying vegetation which was springing up all over the cut area. Leading directly away from the cutover was a little spring creek which emptied into a large creek a mile away. One half mile to the north was another creek and on its north bank was a little pasture covered with burr clover and other favorite pickings of the wild turkey. To the south were three miles of unbroken hardwood ridges with their full complement of spring branches. The main creek was to the west and some three miles to the east was the public highway. It was far back in the woods and I had a good mind's eye picture of the situation as I began to make plans for an encounter with Van's Poor Old Gobbler.

I began by making an afternoon scouting foray. I eased along from one end of the cutover to the other, hoping that the turkey was not home. I never like to encounter a gobbler of this stature until it's to my advantage. It was a scourching hot afternoon. I didn't use my callers at all even though there were gobbler tracks everywhere. I was hoping only to roost the bird.

I reached the head of the spring branch about one hour before sunset. With as little commotion as possible, I crawled up in a dark shadowy clump of bushes and confirmed that I had a relatively quiet exit route. There were no magnolia trees with their noisy brittle leaves between my hiding place and the little trail that ran along the branch back to the main logging road which traveled back to my truck, located one mile away.

I reached for my wingbone caller as the longest shadows began to cross the cutover. Lonesome hen imitations went forth repeatedly, softly; yet loudly as only a wingbone caller will do. For a long time, it appeared that maybe the gobbler was spooked. Was he going to roost on the edge of that little pasture far to the north? Maybe this bird was indeed too wise for all of this foolishness. I stayed put even though the first hour and one half of waiting produced no response from the gobbler.

About thirty minutes before dark, there came a short suspicious sounding gobble from down under the hill, two hundred yards from where I sat. After a short wait, I answered him.

Deafening Silence!

Immediately I made a series of sharp clucks and sat as still as a rock for that final thirty minutes of good daylight. The dusk creatures were stirring when I imitated the fly-up cackle of the hen turkey. As expected, a loud gobble echoed back from the little branch. The tom had not moved five feet from the spot where he had gobbled first.

I slid out of there and walked away from the branch for perhaps four hundred yards. I stopped, looked in the direction of the gobbler, and gave the single note imitation of a barred owl. A shrill rattle came back from the branch. The gathering darkness quickened with my pace along the trail. Upon arriving at the truck which was parked on top of a hill, I could hear a real pair of owls down in there near the branch, laughing and hooting up a storm. The old gobbler was going crazy. The stars were out and he was gobbling his head off. I counted fifty gobbles before I cranked up the truck to head home. Boy, what a fool I thought he was! I knew that I was sitting pretty for the next morning.

At supper, after much bickering with Van, everyone knew exactly where I would be the next morning at gobbling time. The woods would be all mine; Van had to work.

I was up and gone without so much as a cup of coffee the next morning much ahead of regular leaving time. One of those feelings had come over me, you know. There was a heavy dew on the grass and the air felt good. There was no fog and not even a hint of a breeze, the temperature being about fifty degrees.

Because of a little bend in the trail that paralleled the branch, I miscalculated the distance to the gobbler before daylight and the bird was almost directly over my head when daylight came. He began gobbling something fierce and there was no way I could move back without spooking him. I was lucky he didn't see me when I managed to break a small twig about the size of a toothpick while it was still gray light in the hollow. He shut up all that gobbling for a while. It was too dark for him to see the ground under his roost tree when he sailed out to a well lighted ridge two hundred yards away. He remained quiet on the ground for about fifteen minutes. I did no calling and did not move a muscle, while waiting for the duel to begin.

The old tom gobbled softly a time or two. No answer from me. He then began to gobble like he was trying to blow the bark off the trees. Just as I was told, the danged thing would gobble at every living thing which stirred or made a noise.

I moved over and set up on the same ridge with him. An imitation cackle caused him to answer, but he moved again to the next ridge and gobbled ten or twelve times in rapid succession. After circling him, I called again. He answered and moved away, gobbling every few feet of his retreat. The gobbler stopped nearly three hundred yards from me and gobbled five times without drawing a breath. I eased up for a hundred yards and called to him softly, this time changing callers. The monarch double gobbled, circled behind me and gobbled frantically for ten minutes. Wow, what a character he was!

An imitation of an assembly yelp was my next offering. With that he began walking back and forth about two hundred yards out, gobbling once on each end of his beat. From one end of his beat to the other was about seventy five yards.

I retreated to a long point where three little finger ridges came together. After examining the terrain, I cleared the leaves from around the base of an elm tree, quietly. The tree had ferns growing all around it. A gigantic loblolly pine about twenty yards closer to the gobbler caught my attention, so I tipped up and squatted beside it. I looked back at my intended hiding place among the green ferns by the elm tree. It was very hard to see into the ferns from the pine and I was convinced the shadows would stay in there for another two hours. I laid all my callers out in a semicircle around me and thought about things for a minute or two.

By now the gobbler had slowed down his gobbling somewhat and the sounds were not as frantic as they had been earlier. He was close to the cut over, but just inside the canopy of the little branch, standing in an open glade. He must have been very familiar with that spot. The bird was still walking up and down, and he continued to gobble once at each end of his walk.

I picked up the wingbone and held it to my mouth. A minute passed before he gobbled again, whereupon I cut off his gobble with my yelping and kept yelping until the monarch cut me off in return fashion with a passionate gobble. I immediately threw the wingbone down and lit into him with a long series of cutts and assembly yelps with a double staggered reed diaphram. Then I cackled at him with my caller and gobbled at him twice. He cut off my second gobble with an ear splitting reply. "Well good, ol' boy," I whispered.

I picked up all the callers and put them in my hunting vest. The peg and slate was kept handy. The old boy kept up his gobbling exactly one time per minute for the next half hour. He had quit that walking up and down and was now fixed on one spot some two hundred yards from where I squatted.

The next imitation came after that half hour of uninterrupted gobbling. The peg and slate scratched out a very soft cluck and purr. I always wonder if they hear it. This gobbler heard it! I crawled away from the pine and settled into my hiding place among the ferns by the elm tree. I was ready to wait him out.

After removing a couple of bothersome sticks, I double checked my field of view. I sat so I could cover about 160° without moving anything except the end of my shotgun. I shoot left handed. I drew my right knee up and stretched my left leg out flat on the ground. I cleared a few more leaves so I could lean on my right hand from time to time to ease the pressure on my shoulders against the elm tree. I had lots of time.

Regular gobbling continued for another hour, but I said nothing more to the monarch. During the wait, a rather smallish canebrake rattler slid past me and into a hole in the ground behind me. Crows sailing around in the woods worried the old gobbler, and he gobbled at every sound they made.

He had one of those volume control gobbles. Some of his gobbles were not so loud and had a wooden clatter tone to them. Other gobbles were ever so loud and shrill and had a metallic ring to them. Those gobbles intended for the crows were just sort of blurted out. Those aimed at me were carefully measured as if he were saying a phrase or calling someone's name.

Quietly as a breeze, a little hen made her way past me, but not in the direction of the gobbler. That was a good sign, and I knew my wait was nearly over.

Suddenly the woods seemed deathly still, and I realized the cawing crow over near the gobbler had failed to bring a response for the first time . I raised the little .410 to rest on my knee and pulled my cap down over my eyes a little further. Ten minutes passed; I moved only my eyes.

Then I could hear a very faint "tch-tch" two steps at a time approach of the cautious thing. Finally I saw his head, and immediately noticed that his head took on the ash-gray color, the color of suspicion. He came on, "tch-tch", two soft steps and a one minute pause to look closely at every thing around him. He was within thirty yards of me before I could see his whole body. What a grand devil he was, carrying a long slender beard, and having an elongated body symmetry. "Tch", he took only one step behind the big pine where I had called from. I DID NOT MOVE A MUSCLE. I DID NOT EVEN BLINK. Just as I thought, he pulled his head back from behind the pine for another ten second security check. "Tch, tch", two more steps and I brought my weapon to bear on a point beyond the pine where I planned to kill him. He stood stock still in my sights for about three minutes. Slowly his head colors took on the red, white, and blue tones of passion. His mood began to be a little more vain—"Pfffffftt!", a forward snap of his wings produced half a strut. When he stretched his neck to observe the results of himself, I touched off the barrel loaded with 7½s.

I must admit that I enjoy seeing big gobblers drop in their tracks, but I quickly stepped over there and placed the small of my boot across his neck. I also have to admit there is always a touch of sadness inside of me as I watch that magical something fade from fallen gobblers as they stretch their feathers for the last time.

There were several points of interest in this encounter. I suppose the fact that I was familiar with this turkey's neck of the woods enabled me to avoid him and not encounter him on his terms during the afternoon scouting mission. I felt sure he wouldn't be out in the cut over since it was a hot afternoon. How was I to know that he would be in that nice cool little hollow and not a half a mile away on the shady edge of the pasture where he had been so many times during the season?

Well, the old boy had been hunted hard, it was a really hot afternoon, and it was late in the season; all reliable indicators that he might have returned to his main little branch head for roosting.

You see, if someone told me they would give me a million dollars to go find a big gobbler, I would begin my search at any time of the year on any range of the little spring branches way back in the woods. You might find them visiting the field edges, the big fine hardwood ridges, or even in your back yards sometimes. But I'll tell you that classy gobblers live on the little spring fed creeks and branches for the most part.

The reason I made the sharp clucks after I got the reluctant answer in the afternoon is that the turkey didn't sound like he was coming to my call; you can just tell after a while. I just wanted to let him know that I was a little suspicious too and it has been my experience that sharp clucks will at least make old gobblers stretch their necks and look and listen from the same spot for a while. I guessed the careful bird I was foolin' with would spend that last half hour of daylight looking and listening from the same spot rather than walking a mile down the branch to roost somewhere else. When he began his gobbling at dark, I knew that the gamble had paid off.

Wild gobblers are scared of almost everything. I made the faint snapping of a tiny twig just to put a little something in the turkey's head so he would fly down away from the roost tree and into an area of good light. If he had flown down in that dark hollow where both he and I were, he most likely would have seen me within seconds. He did fly out on the well lighted ridge and could not see me in the darkened hollow.

Long hard gobbling toms will generally work best if you give them something to really gobble about; that's why I made all the callers work for me. However, it is almost always true that these *noisy types*, some used to calling hens, also need to have the last word. So, with a real gobbling turkey, just get him in a frenzy by interrupting his gobbling and then just quit calling and wait. It is well documented that however simple or stupid a bird may be, he does know exactly where you are after you call. Please note that the gobbler in this episode came directly to the pine where I had done all that calling.

It is customary for old gobblers, and some younger ones, especially those whose heads are momentarily ash-gray in hue, to step behind a tree and then peek out again for another look. That's why I didn't get my gun up as soon as the turkey went behind the tree. I'm not saying they are such clever things, but I am saying that these little habits of theirs is one reason the rank and file hunting club member cannot kill them consistently by calling them up fair and square.

Let me point out here that all old gobblers have one or two peculiarities all their own. Good hunters will just have to learn to deal with them. I have come across a number of wild gobblers with such peculiar habits as to make them almost unkillable by sporting means. I'm sure you will find some like that too.

Van's turkey was a real thrill for me. The turkey put on a great show, he was a classy looking bird, and I bagged him fair and square on his own turf way back in the woods. The beauty of the deep woods in the spring makes a hunt worthwhile even if the gobblers don't cooperate.

* * * * *

Miscellaneous Facts/Opinions

The wild turkey is native to these United States. The domesticated turkey which was re-introduced here came from the Mexican stock and not from the Eastern Wild Turkey, *Meleagris gallapavo sylvestris*. The eastern wild turkey has never been domesticated although it does adapt to the presence of human beings.

The Florida wild turkey may be considered a separate race from the eastern wild turkey, but the two races have long been known to interbreed wherever they come in contact. The early descriptions of the two races indicate that birds need to be examined under laboratory conditions in order to tell them apart.

* * * * *

"A few trophies"

"The Hillside Running Technique"

2 Gobbler on a Ledge

During the late winter and early spring of 1979, I had the same horrible nightmare every night for thirty straight nights. I dreamed that I was a big old gobbler trapped up on a high bluff by an angry crowd of deer hunters. There was no way to escape except to sail off the ledge, but I couldn't. My wings did not have any flight feathers. I would always wake up just before I jumped or before the mob got to me.

In reality, I was having a low grade fever of about 100° every night. I was sick and none of the local doctors could diagnose what was wrong with me. I must have consumed ten gallons of medicine, and I was not feeling any better. And turkey season was about to open.

At four thirty in the morning on opening day, I checked my temperature; it was 101°. I began to get prepared to go turkey hunting. My wife protested and begged me to stay home and keep my doctor's appointment. But William Yarbrough of our turkey hunting fraternity had located a whole gang of gobbling turkeys with his directional listening devices and I was determined to make the opening morning hunt.

I went to a place which was very easy to hunt. I could drive close to where a turkey had been gobbling, and I could make a little relaxed hunt and then go to the doctor. I had a special bottle of cough syrup to deal with the severe cough I had developed.

As luck would have it, I got hooked up at daylight with a *vagabond* type of gobbler. I didn't feel like chasing the thing all over the country, but I did. There were two gobblers roosting pretty close together. They both gobbled a few times on the roost. Another gobbler was sounding off far to the north and yet another was gobbling half a mile to the east.

I got the attention of the closest gobbler very early, and he flew down within a hundred yards of me. I could see him plainly, and he is one of the very few turkeys I have ever seen go into a full strut upon landing on the ground without stretching his neck and taking a short security check. I mean he was strutting almost before he came to a stop on the open hickory ridge across the hollow from me.

I called to him on the ground over there; he broke strut and gobbled. Then he began a slow walk down the ridge away from me. About every fifty feet he would pause, gobble, strut for a minute or so, and then continue on down the ridge which paralleled a big creek. I could hear the other close turkey about four hundred yards from me. That one sounded like he had flown down on the sandbar of the big creek.

When my gobbler was well out of sight, I crossed the hollow. The ravine which I crossed was straight up and down. On the other side, I felt a coughing spasm coming on and I took a big swig of the cough syrup. I had to cough a little anyway, and I buried my head in my hunting cap to do so. I finally got squared away and listened for the gobbler so I could decide what to do next.

When he gobbled again, he had gone a quarter of a mile down that ridge. Of course I got up and followed him. I approached as close as I dared and cackled at him. He answered, but I could tell he was still moving away from me to the south. After a few minutes, I offered another cackle. "Cut-tabba-tabba-tabba", shot back to me from the south. He had almost reached the end of the ridge. Maybe he would come back; the terrain beyond where he answered was very rough and much of it was a jungle of thick undergrowth.

About fifteen minutes of silence followed. All the turkeys in this part of the world had grown quiet. This area's gobblers have long been known for shutting up early. This particular flock of turkeys has been thriving in the area since before I was born and they are among the wildest of any birds anywhere. They are the original ones.

I cackled again and the gobbler answered; he was already in the thick stuff. I had a hard time making up my mind what to do next. There was not much desire in me to follow him around in that two hundred acre thicket of ravines and sink holes. I decided to circle around. I got underway; there was a mile of walking ahead of me.

Another coughing spell came over me just about the time I got in my next "encounter area". I took a couple of big swallows of "the stuff" and found a good place to hide. I was sweating profusely, and my head was hurting as if somebody were sticking needles in my brain. I began to wonder if I might not have been really crazy or something for being out there with such a sickness gripping me.

The turkey gobbled shortly thereafter, less than two hundred yards from where I had set up. My headache went away. He answered my next cackle by double gobbling. He gobbled another time after a two minute pause. A soft yelp brought an immediate response. I got ready.

Thirty minutes later the old gobbler sounded off at least four hundred yards still further south. I felt very discouraged. After struggling to my feet and walking to the top of the ridge to the south, I thought very seriously about giving up. The longbeard taunted me with another gobble; he was really getting a far piece to the south. But I could tell that he was alone; he just sort of said as much every time he gobbled. My mind was made up; I would follow him as long as I could.

We had moved yet another mile to the south before another hour passed. The gobbler was out on a big sand bar just walking around doing nothing that I could see. From my vantage point on a bluff overlooking the creek, I began by imitating the lonesome yelp of a hen. He gobbled back and continued to mill around out there like a school boy waiting on the corner for his date.

Another fifteen minutes or so had passed. The long ranky rascal suddenly darted away and disappeared into the woods on the other side of the creek. I could not believe how fast the turkey ran across some shallow pools of water. He did not even make the water splash. The turkey employed the "hillside running technique", a procedure gobblers use on open ground by lifting their wings parallel to the ground and half-spreading their tail feathers creating an airfoil. While running like this, their feet churn almost too fast for the human eye to follow. This gobbler's head was stretched out low to the ground and cocked to one side so he could survey the ground he was swallowing up as he sped along.

A full minute passed before I heard the three-wheelers coming up the creek, the objects which had caused the gobbler to run. And it was nearly five minutes before the boys on the three wheelers got up to the spot where the turkey had been milling around on the sand bar. These fellows were not hunting, and they continued on up the creek. Soon they were out of hearing.

I felt like they had ruined my chances of bagging the gobbler on this particular morning. Another gulp of cough medicine later and I was beginning to think about the two mile hike back to my truck. I decided that I ought to rest a few minutes before starting back. It really was a pleasant morning, and the medicine had me feeling not so poorly as before.

Suddenly the gobbler appeared back out on the sand bar. He had had the presence of mind to just get out of sight of the three wheelers until they passed. He acted as if he were accustomed to getting spooked off the sand bar.

Immediately, I called to him; he fixed his wings over his back and marched straight across the creek, wading through the water until it was up to his leg feathers and then flop-flopping the rest of the way across.

He was on my side of the creek, and I have never felt more confident of killing a gobbler in my life. I raised my shotgun to my knee even though the turkey was still a long distance down in the woods. I waited and waited and waited. Thirty minutes later he gobbled on his own, some four hundred yards still further to the south. He continued to work away from me, gobbling as he went.

The woods made a bend with the creek down there where he was heading, and I thought that he just might stay with the lay of the land. By walking east, I could intercept him again within the next hour. It had been three hours since he gobbled on the roost, and I did not know how far the durn thing would travel in the next three hours. It began to appear that the gobbler was going to walk into town.

I had another mile of walking ahead of me, but I was consoled by the fact that my new place was not any further from the truck. Since I was not feeling any worse, I became more determined than ever to get this bird. I do remember wishing that I had set up to call the tom which had sailed down on the sand bar early that morning instead of going after this vagabond critter.

Upon arrival at the next setup, I figured it was better to let the turkey announce his arrival before I did any calling. When he did gobble, he was north of me in the direction of my truck. My reply he did not answer. How aggravating gobblers can be at times!

The turkey was directly between me and my truck. There was a little opening somewhere over in there too. I hadn't been to that opening in years, but I knew where it was. I headed there, post haste.

I was through with my coughing for the day—apparently; and no wonder, I had consumed half a bottle of cough syrup. I was somewhat intoxicated and was feeling no pain at all. In fact, a real happy feeling had engulfed me.

When the opening was spotted, a wave of disappointment came over me. The clearing had grown up thick with briars and weeds almost as high as a man's head. No chance of waiting for the turkey at this spot so I headed for the truck.

Suddenly the bird gobbled just off to the east. I dropped to one knee and called softly—no answer. In a few moments here came the turkey. His head was red, white, and blue, and he was a reddish colored turkey, an erythristic color pattern. He was not the *oceola* variety; I could see the prominent barring on his wing primaries.

I could not understand why he was marching so straight to me until I finally saw the little hen walking ahead of him. The hen veered off to my right, and I called at her using the conversational yelp. She yelped back, and the gobbler followed her to his death. He did a complete flip forward when I shot him, landing on his feet and just standing there for a full minute. He began his death flop while he was still on his feet—unusual to say the least.

The turkey had walked in a huge circle, thankfully all the way back to my truck. My headache returned with a vengeance, and my cough was back. I was completely exhausted when I got in the truck.

The appointment my wife had made for me was with a new doctor, Larry Schneider, of St. Francisville. I arrived at his office just as they were closing for the day. The doctor happened to be out in the waiting room. He kind of looked at me funny and told me to come right on in. After the examination, he gave me a grim report. He informed me that I was very likely going to die if I didn't check into the hospital. I tried to explain about turkey season being open, but his argument was fairly convincing about all the dying and stuff. I checked into the hospital convinced that I was going to miss my first turkey season since Vietnam. Dr. Schneider didn't know what was wrong with me, but he vowed to get me well again.

I was finally diagnosed as having Brucellosis, a disease normally transmitted to humans by drinking untreated milk from cows carrying the disease. I had not drunk any milk like that for twenty years. The other sources of the disease come from handling animals which might have the sickness. I did handle a deer earlier that year which had died from unknown reasons.

My stay in the hospital was agony. All the turkey hunting gang would come by and keep me posted on the progress of the season. I was miserable, but the fraternity did a lot to keep my attitude right. One morning, Lu Howell brought an exceptional gobbler to the hospital. The bird had about a twelve inch beard and spurs nearly one and a half inches long. He created quite a stir by placing the gobbler up in the window of the hospital room.

William Yarbrough came every morning and read the newspaper while we listened to the recordings he made every morning, with the fine recording equipment he had to go with the directional microphone. William would put a long blank tape on the recorder every morning before daylight at one of our many favorite places. After setting up the recorder and turning on the whole apparatus, he would leave the area and drive to another area to hunt. By returning and picking up the tape, we could listen to what kind of gobbling went on where no one was hunting. He recorded some excellent live sounds.

One morning, we were listening to some pretty gobbler talk which had been recorded in the "south end" part of our hunting lease. Suddenly the loud report from a shotgun interrupted the gobbling noises we were listening to. William and I sat up and took note. A poacher? We didn't know anyone who was supposed to be hunting in that area on this morning. As you might know, we were a little bit disturbed. No more gobbles could be heard on that particular tape.

Some investigation by Butch Trahan, one of our regular hunters, revealed that our neighbor to the west had been hunting in the area. The man claimed to have been on his own place. William, who is an attorney with a District Attorney's office, pointed out to the man that the directional microphone could not possibly have picked up the shot so clearly if he had been on his side of the fence. The guy finally admitted to crossing the fence. He had heard that I was in the hospital and did not think anybody would be around.

We assured him that he would have been welcomed to go hunting if he had only asked permission. The guy shot at a gobbler, but did not get the turkey. He was trying to sneak up on a turkey which was gobbling on the roost. Ain't that a shame for a grown man to not only trespass on private property, but to try to shoot a gobbler off the roost?

I continued to heal, but the doctor claimed that I would have to stay in bed for at least a month after I left the hospital. There were less than two weeks of turkey season left. I began to plot ways to get back out into the woods. My wife can sense when I am up to something and scolded me for not obeying the doctor's orders, even before I failed to obey the orders. I assured her that I was going to be a good patient.

When Linda would go to work in the mornings, after I got out of the hospital, she would call every couple of hours to see if I were really resting as ordered. I really started feeling a lot better with six days left in the turkey season. All that good home cooking and rest and relaxation seemed to be just what I needed. I came up with the perfect plan for getting back at the turkeys.

For three straight afternoons, Butch's brother-in-law, Keith Thompson would come by the house in his bronco, and we would go looking for turkeys. We spotted several. They did not seem to mind the bronco very much, and we looked at some real nice gobblers in the field edges every afternoon. It's amazing how wild turkeys are more afraid of some vehicles than they are others. My yellow pickup scares the hell out of them, while my old black truck doesn't bother them at all.

I had plans of making another hunt before the season was over. I knew though, that I could not walk more than two hundred yards without collapsing. William came up with the perfect gobbler for me to hunt. He had been fooling with that gobbler on the sand bar where I had begun the season. William insisted that I go down there and get the gobbler. There would be very little walking involved in getting at this gobbler. Now all we had to do was get by Linda and out into the woods with my shotgun.

I invited William to stay at our house for the remainder of the turkey season since he was planning on hunting every day anyway. This would be a good excuse for me to get up in the mornings. We did this for a couple of mornings, and I would lie down on the couch after the hunters left for the morning hunt. Invariably, Linda would come in the living room just to reassure herself that I was in there. I was betting she would not come and check until it was too late on the final weekend. She liked to sleep late on Saturdays anyway. It worked.

When William left for the turkey woods on the Saturday morning with all his customary banging around, I just followed him outside with my shotgun and hunting stuff. I got in the truck with Bob Price, and we drove off. William went after another gobbler, but Bob and I headed for the sandbar gobbler which roosted on a big bluff overlooking the creek. Bob drove down to the bluff where the old gobbler hung out; his little truck was very quiet, and it was a long time before daylight.

I instructed Bob not to return for me until he heard a shot.

It was a fine morning and I really did feel good. At daylight the old gobbler on the bluff sounded off a couple of times and then sailed out to the sand bar, like a big eagle. He gobbled and strutted, and gobbled and strutted some more. Two hens came to visit him and left. He remained on the sand bar strutting and gobbling. I was about one hundred and fifty yards from the turkey. Down the creek from the gobbler was a big sycamore and several other trees with wide crowns. These trees were growing directly out of the creek bank. It was still early, but I saw the shady spot under those trees already beginning to form. It was a little warm for even the early morning as it was near the end of April. I stalked back into the woods so the gobbler could not hear or see me and walked down the creek to a spot on top of the bluff near the clump of shade trees.

I looked up the creek and the old gobbler was still out there on the big sand bar. Two jakes came out there and he chased them around a little while. Another hen finally joined the big gobbler, so I gave a soft yelp. Both the hen and the gobbler stretched their necks, looked in my direction and then went back to their respective tasks, the hen picking grit and the gobbler remaining in a full strut.

As soon as the rising sun coming up over the bluff made the gobbler look shiny, I got my gun up on my knee. I pointed it at the middle of the patch of shade in front of me. The patch of shade was just about thirty yards from me, straight down from the top of the bluff where I sat perched and ready for action. The sand bar was glistening white now and I knew it would not be long before the moment of truth. The creek was only about ten yards wide at this point.

The hen and the gobbler made their way in my direction. Both of the turkeys parked themselves in the shade across the creek. They would look at themselves in the water and periodically each would pick up a small pebble on the sandy little beach. The gobbler remained in a big round ball the whole time in the cool of the shade. I could have killed him at any time. I observed the pair for nearly an hour, because I did not want to have to walk down under that bluff to get him. I had decided to kill him right where he stood if they started to leave in the other direction. I was hoping they would cross back to my side of the creek.

They did exactly that. The hen flop-flopped across the creek and came straight up the bluff like a mountain goat. The gobbler also made the flop-flop across, but waited at the base of the bluff. When the hen was just below the rim of the bluff, with nothing but her head sticking up, she suspended herself there for a long moment and took a look around. I did not move and she hopped up on the top of the bank and started off through the woods.

The gobbler started up. He was not as agile as the hen, but was making the climb OK. When he peeked his head over the top, he also paused to look the situation over. I had the gun on him. His head vanished for a moment and with my heart in my throat, he suddenly hopped up on the bank. He made a few very fast steps and then stopped and looked, standing erect and still for a second. That was his last look. I sure wish he hadn't flopped back over the edge of that bluff.

I was amazed at not being tired after retrieving the gobbler with a mountain climbing exercise which was necessary. I felt fine, never better in fact. He was a fine gobbler and I don't think I will ever appreciate hunting one more than I did this one. Of course, Linda was furious when we got home—she got over it though.

* * * * *

Miscellaneous Facts/Opinions

As recorded by Iberville, an early explorer in our part of the country, the sound of "Turkey Cocks" was a deafening roar on spring mornings. This indicates the bird must have been quite plentiful as a purely woodland species.

Only live trapped birds of wild origin have been successfully used to restore flocks on part of the turkey's range. The pen raised stock used in some places did not fare well at all and died out soon after they were stocked into an area.

Spring turkey seasons are often set according to politics and sometimes have little to do with sound biological reasons given by game biologists. This needs to change for the good of the turkey.

* * * * *

"Ketch 'Im"

3 Buster and Dad

Since there was alway a new BB gun or something under the tree at Christmas time, Mom and Dad, being the practical people they were, managed to have us get our stuff on Christmas Eve rather than wait for morning. We always had a little surprise in the morning, but those practical gifts were ready to go at first light on Christmas Day. On one special Christmas Eve, my long box under the tree seemed a bit too heavy to be another daisy pump and I paced up and down waiting for my dad to get home from the dairy.

At last he arrived, and in a short while we were ready to open the gifts. In my box was a brand new single barrelled twenty gauge shotgun. It was just what the doctor ordered. At last I could graduate from the little 22 rifle I was allowed to shoot "short" ammunition with. I could just imagine all kinds of game winding up on our table as a result of this fine gift.

After supper, Dad announced that we were going on a hunting trip the next day over at his home place near the little settlement of Felixville, Louisiana on the Amite River. He wanted to see his brother and friends as well as to try out the new squirrel dog we had.

We left long before daylight and the thirty minute ride was laced with one lecture after another about shotguns, safety, squirrel dogs, and about being nice to all those old people at Felixville. We had a great time and the Christmas dinner Mrs. Lily Delee fixed us was well worth being polite for.

Earlier in the day we had a fine hunt. By nine o'clock we had sixteen squirrels, eight swamp rabbits, a couple of wood ducks, a merganzer, a mallard, and some woodcock. Buster turned out to be a dog of all trades. I must admit the dog and Dad were the most effective game collectors that I ever saw. To this day I have never seen anyone to equal my dad as a trapper and hunter.

What happened next on that hunt borders on the unbelievable. Dad nor I fired another shot that day.

We were walking up an old log road and I was literally staggering under the great load of game Dad had saddled me with. I was complaining about how heavy it was and Dad was laughing and explaining how lucky we were to have not killed any coons way back there in that swamp. Those coons could really be heavy. Dad did agree to carry anything else which we might happen to stumble upon.

Suddenly, Buster let out one of those little short barks of surprise. A tremendous racket boiled up out of the thicket where the dog was and Dad yelled, "Ketch 'im!". I thought the dog had hold of a deer or something. In a few moments, a big gobbler flew up out of the thicket with the little dog hanging on to one of his feet. After a flight of seventy yards or so, the gobbler and the dog came to the ground again and another loud commotion ensued. We dropped everything and ran to the scene of the fight. By the time we got there, we knew that either the dog or the turkey was dead because everything was quite still.

My dad was so proud of that little ol' stinking dog—the dog had killed a twenty pound gobbler and from that day on, Dad let Buster sleep with him and Mom.

Some really strange things used to happen out there at Felixville, still do, so I am told. One time Dad and I were out there on Big Beaver Creek specifically for the purpose of killing a big old gobbler. We peeked out in this man's field and there stood a fine gobbler, pecking in a pile of feed the man had left for his cows. "He's too far", I whispered over Dad's shoulder. "Blam!", went Dad's old gun and away flew the gobbler.

I was just beginning to get on Dad's nerves with my, "I told you so", comments when the sudden flopping of a dying turkey could be heard from beyond the thicket. The bird had done some amazing acrobatics while flying through the thickets and did not appear hurt at all after the shot.

Later at home, my brother Wade picked the turkey from top to bottom and announced that there were no shot holes anywhere in the turkey. Everybody examined the carcass and we all reached the same conclusion. Uncle Russell said that the gobbler must have died of a heart attack. It was the only explanation until someone spotted a sewing pin sized hole just under the gobbler's eye. Careful dissection revealed an inch long cedar stick imbedded in the turkey's brain. The gobbler must have impaled himself when he flew through the thicket. Dad is also a lucky hunter.

At the writing of this book, there was some opposition from some members of the family about telling too many of Dad's secrets and about some of his experiences. Some things must be forever a secret within this family. However, I would like to tell about one more adventure which Dad and I had in the "good old days".

The Game and Fish Agency in Louisiana used to give out tags to be attached to dead turkeys and deer. Each hunter had to immediately tag a downed animal. Pity the unfortunate guy coming out of the woods with an untagged turkey. I recall one season when each licensed hunter got two tags for turkeys. Let's see, Dad got two, Mom got two, my sister got two, each of my brothers got two, and of course, I got two tags also. I think I am correct in recalling that the Morgan family had twelve turkey tags, collectively, that spring. Springtime is a beautiful time of the year—Ah Yes!

Of course Buster stayed locked up all spring. He didn't have any turkey tags and we could never make the fool dog understand that we wanted the turkeys left alone. I could never figure out why he would go crazy everytime he saw one, dead or alive. Mom said the dog acted just like his owner.

Somehow, near the last part of the season, we had only one unused tag left and somehow it had Dad's name on it. I really felt like I had been taken advantage of. Mom and Sis never even left the house with their tags.

But Dad talked me into making an afternoon hunt with him just to witness the killing of a big bronze gobbler up at a place we called the "stump field". A wary old monarch had been ringing the woods up there and had somehow lived long enough to grow a foot long beard and long curved spurs. The gobbler had the habit of taking off in the opposite direction of anyone who called to him and disappearing for two or three days at a time. It had been a week since anyone had been up there and Dad figured we could catch the gobbler out in the stump field late that evening.

I agreed to go with Dad and take part in this 'finale' hunt of the season. There were some serious words between Dad and me before he finally agreed for me to take a gun. He handed me a little old .410

shotgun which had a bent barrel. The barrel had become bent hitting a possum over the head and I did not think it would kill a gobbler. I was furious, but I went on with Dad anyway.

The gobbler was in the field, as predicted. Dad whispered my instructions as we watched the bird strut around and around under some trees out in the field. I was to slip around to the opposite side of the field and sing out with a couple of yelps on my switch cane caller, then sit still or go back to the truck; Dad didn't care which. He was going to take care of the rest.

Dad doesn't believe it 'til this day, but when I got to the other side of the field, I forgot about the cane caller being in my back pocket. I sat on it and broke it half in two, and all I could do was sit there and watch the gobbler.

As my good fortune, or bad fortune, would have it, the danged old turkey walked within twenty feet of where I was hiding. I had to shoot the gobbler in self defense and took dead aim at the gobbler's head with the bent barrelled .410. I had to run the turkey down after shooting him, but he wound up quite dead all the same.

About the time I got the turkey's feathers all fixed pretty after the bird quit flopping, up walks Dad. I'll tell you that I have never seen that kind of look on Dad's face before or since. It was a real hurt look, but mad too. Dad said, "Well, shit." I didn't say anything—I knew better. Finally Dad just walked off in the direction of the truck.

My troubles had just begun. At the sound of the shot, George Bunch, the local game warden, had driven down the road where he was patrolling and parked by Dad's truck. And Dad being in the state of mind that he was, had walked off and left me with a dead turkey and no turkey tag. Fortunately Dad had the mercy to steer the game warden away from there. He told George to come on over to the house and have a cup of coffee.

They must have had more than coffee, because it was midnight before Dad came back to get me. He seemed to be in a lot better humor than he was when I last saw him. The only thing more he had to say about the killing of the bronze gobbler was, "Don't ever do anything like that again". Of course I replied, "I won't do it anymore, Daddy".

Wild gobblers will sometimes make you do and say things that you don't mean.

* * * * *

Miscellaneous Facts/Opinions

It is hunting pressure which makes a turkey extremely wild and cautious, not the locale where it is found. We all like to believe that we are hunting the wildest creature on earth and if the gobbler gives one the slip, he indeed is the wildest thing one ever saw.

Most animals, including wild turkey, reach heavier sizes in the northern parts of their range. Some modern day flocks are made up of heavier adults because of this phenomenon and other adults are heavier because of the "hybrid vigor" exhibited by the wide range within the gene pool brought about by the restocking program. An adult gobbler of the South averages less than twenty pounds in weight and the turkeys farther north probably exceed the twenty pound standard on a regular basis.

Although most American Indian tribes depended upon the wild turkey for food, clothing, ornaments, and weaponry, some groups of our aborigines shunned the use of the turkey. Apparently those few groups preferred fish and red meat over the whiter flesh of the turkey.

Various color phases of the wild turkey exist. Some are reddish, some yellowish, some are melanistic (blackish) and others are even partially or totally white. These color phases do not indicate impurities of domestic origin, but recessive gene expression which is present in all wild flocks.

* * * * *

"A Poor Choice of Shots"

4 A Mid Day Gobbler to Remember

About twenty years ago a man who owned a pretty piece of property near our farm came by our dairy barn one afternoon to discuss some business with my dad. During the lengthy conversation between the two men, I seized upon the opportunity to ask the man for permission to hunt turkeys on his place. The spring gobbling season was close at hand. Our good neighbor's answer, in effect, told me that I most certainly could hunt, but he didn't want me out there hunting while he was present on the property. He wanted to kill a gobbler himself.

I suggested that we could go together, that I could call real good and that we each could get a nice gobbler. "No, no," the man held fast and repeated his conditions about my hunting on his place. I thanked him politely, throwing in a little diversionary remark about how busy I was and that I probably wouldn't be able to hunt much anyway.

The man's place just had to be wrapped up in turkeys. He was such an ornery old soul, surely no one else had bothered the turkeys out there for years. Of course, I didn't tell him that he was an ornery old soul.

I began observing the habits of the man first, and discovered that he hunted every morning from daylight until about nine o'clock. He would then leave and go to town during the midday hours. He returned every afternoon and stayed in a blind at the edge of a pasture where he hunted until dark.

My primary plans had been to wait for him to be absent on any morning and then go in there and get after the turkeys. However, the man stuck to his routine and I resolved that I would have to go in the middle of the day while the man was in town. In passing, I would talk to the man about turkey hunting. He told me all about the turkeys he had been seeing from his blind, and about hearing four or five different turkeys gobbling every morning.

I was waiting just down the road when he left his place for town on about the fifth or sixth morning of the season. Since he had made it known that he was using the blind in the edge of the pasture, I figured that was where all the action was. The man owned nearly one thousand acres, but I headed straight for that pasture.

The pasture was growing thick with little yellow topped clover of the genus *Medicago*. It was a burr clover which all the local farmers called hop clover. It is one of the wild turkey's favorite forage foods both before and after the little plants go to seed. In all the years that I have hunted turkeys, I have never seen any kind of field plant which turkeys prefer over this clover. They would rather eat burr clover than crimson clover any day.

There were lots of turkey tracks around the pasture, but none of the birds were present at that time of the day. I left the pasture and headed for the biggest block of woods on the whole one thousand acres. Real turkey woods were what I found and turkey sign was literally everywhere I looked. Since it was my habit to use the middle of the day for scouting, I really wasn't in the killing frame of mind. I just ambled along, never even took my callers out, and did not sit down once.

Before I left the place, I had walked up on several little groups of turkeys. I was encouraged and made a lot of mental notes about what to do when I did get in a killing frame of mind. The best gobbler that I saw was standing on top of a long hill where two ridges came together. I knew from the way his crown cap tilted to the side, making him look as though he were wearing a beret, that he was an old turkey.

Late that afternoon, I went to visit Mr. Ellis Hopkins, formerly of Livingston Parish, an employee at the hospital in Jackson, and an experienced old hunter who had become my coach. I told him of all my findings and Mr. Hopkins was always a good listener. He was a good talker too, and our conversation lasted until well after dark.

Mr. Hopkins informed me that a hunter had to hide much more thoroughly during the midday and afternoon hours because a turkey could see so much better then than during the early morning time. Mr. Hopkins also told me that all the old turkeys he had ever found in the middle of the day were at their spot the same time of the day, day after day, and year after year. I thought about the old gobbler with the beret on his head. Surely this old turkey had been coming up on that hill every day for a long time.

The next day at ten o'clock, I headed straight for the hill where I had seen the old monarch. I was much more careful now and approached the hill slowly, quietly, and through the thickest wax myrtle tangle on earth.

When I was about one hundred yards from the top of the hill, and still buried in the wax myrtles, I paused to think about the situation. The thought of the turkeys' ability to see so well late up in the day had me in a tentative posture about walking out in the open. I figured I had better call from the thicket down under the hill. I was literally buried in the cover, but I could see the entire slope which led down to where I was parked in the bushes.

At my first call, I was completely surprised to hear a thin high voiced gobble come back to me. The gobbler had to be less than one hundred and twenty five yards away and his immediate response indicated that he was definitely interested. In less than five minutes, the old tom appeared on top of the hill; he had two other gobblers with him and they were dragging ten or eleven inch beards too.

The old turkey was the only one to strut, but eventually all three began to answer my lonesome yelps. First the old one would gobble and then the other two would gobble in unison. The trio stayed up there all afternoon and no amount of anything could get them down off that hill. I quit calling eventually. The gobblers would leave for a while and then come back to the top of the hill, all on their own accord, mind you, without any encouragement from me.

Finally, the man arrived in his blind at the edge of the pasture back to the east of me about half a mile. I heard him slam the truck door. I decided to stay put all afternoon and whatever happened, I was not going to shoot anything. I didn't want any hard feelings to crop up between me and Dad and this man.

The gobblers never strayed too far from the top of the hill until about an hour before sunset when they disappeared without a clue. I slipped away and made plans for another encounter. There was only one thing to do. Get up there on top of that hill and wait. My young mind was frantic as I made foolish plans of building a blind up there on top of that hill. All I could think of was how open the woods were and how well the gobblers could see.

At ten o'clock the next day, I was approaching the hill again—cautiously. In spite of my careful manner, the turkeys were standing in a shady spot and saw me before I saw them. They ran off like they expected me to come slipping up there; not in too big of a hurry but just getting on away from me.

Although thoroughly disgusted, I decided to use my time to build a blind. No fewer than two hundred of the wax myrtles from down under the hill were used and the blind looked like a beaver lodge when completed. I dragged a big hickory limb up into the network of the blind and found that my shotgun would rest perfectly on the limb just at eye level when I sat in the blind. I was ready—the ignorance of youth is a wonder.

I sat in the blind, just to practice sitting in it, until dark. Even I knew the gobblers weren't coming back that day. At about five o'clock a shot rang out from the clover pasture. This caused me to squirm a little and wonder what was going on over there with the man and the blind and the gobblers.

That night, I casually dropped by the man's house to see what had taken place. He informed me that three big gobblers had walked right up to his blind while he was taking a nap. He raised his gun to shoot, the gobblers started running off, and he fired anyway. The man presented me with a handful of the black feathers from a gobbler's lower back. He had hit one of the turkeys, but did not get the bird. The turkey which had been hit was reported to have rolled over on the ground and then got up and flew off. The other two birds just ran across the pasture and had even stopped for a short while on the other side of the pasture. Then they went back into the woods. I didn't know what to think.

The next day, I sat in my new blind anyway—all day long, and did not see a single turkey. The performance was repeated the day after that and I was beginning to wear a hole in the ground in the middle of my blind.

On the third day at noon, I saw the three gobblers slipping toward me cautiously. One of the younger gobblers looked like he had been pulled through a washing machine ringer backwards. The trio milled around about seventy-five yards from the blind. They refused to come any closer and there were no strutting parades going on. Every once in a while, as if by common agreement, all three of the birds would stare for long moments in my direction.

I had already made my mind up that I was going to dismantle this blind as soon as the turkeys left. I didn't have long to wait because the gobblers did not stay around long. They were not even out of sight good when I began dismantling the blind, and carrying the material back down to the bottom of the hill. I was getting a complex like only a turkey hunter can get.

It didn't matter that I was having some good morning hunts elsewhere. The turkeys apparently had an agreement with the man who owned the property to make me look pitifully inept. I found myself wishing I could tell that one gobbler how ridiculous he looked with all his feathers so rumpled up after being shot in the butt by a man with a box caller who sat in a blind in the edge of a pasture.

I stayed away from there several days and tried to regain some of my composure. I even went back to eating and sleeping like a regular person while another plan had begun to become formulated.

The next time I tried the gobblers on the hill, a repeat performance of my very first calling exercise was necessary. Again the old gobbler answered me while I was hiding in the thicket at the bottom of the hill and once more he arrived at the top of the hill in less than five minutes. The other two gobblers were still with him and everything had returned to normal, apparently.

Now my plans were quite clear. Tommorow I would call from the bottom of the hill, get the answer, race to the top of the hill, lay flat on my stomach for five short minutes, and simply blow the turkey's brains out when he came to me. It was such a simple plan I wondered why I hadn't thought of it before. Sometimes the simple things in life are so hard for us to master.

Well, when it came time to execute my perfect plan the next day, I did something which is common to all contestants in many kinds of contests. I CHOKED! The gobbler did not answer my call and this bothered me so much until I froze at the bottom of the hill. I thought he must have been gone or something.

The gobblers, even though they didn't answer, marched boldly up on the hill again. There I was like a big dummy buried in the wax myrtle thicket. I reached deep inside of me and fought back the great temptation to go charging up the hill, screaming Indian war cries with my shotgun blazing away. No—I calmed myself by eating the wax myrtle leaves which hung all around my face as I watched the old one strut all over the top of that hill.

I got the diarrhea from eating the wax myrtle leaves. My mood must have been reflected plainly, because later on Dad looked at me quizzically out of the corner of his eye for about ten minutes. My mother kept patting me on the head and telling me that everything was going to be all right. I couldn't sleep at all that night as I wrestled with the thought of the gobbler outdoing me.

I finally convinced myself that I really didn't care whether I killed that old turkey or not. I decided that if I ever went turkey hunting again, I would just relax and would try to have some fun.

It was easy to make all these resolutions without the big old gobbler staring me in the face. I was after him hot and heavy again the next day, but I did take on a little bit different outlook. I did not feel as if I were under so much pressure as before. I had actually half convinced myself that it really didn't matter too much.

Right on schedule, I left the road at ten o'clock and eased along through the entire length of the man's place. I wasn't going any place in particular and had no appointments to keep. By noon I had called up several gobblers including a big bronze three year old bird. For some reason, I just didn't shoot any of the turkeys I saw. I was wondering why I hadn't shot when I reached the bottom of that hill. I knew—I wanted to kill the old tom with the beret on his head.

Out of habit, I made the lonesome yelp at the bottom of the hill. No answer. I casually walked to the top of the hill and slouched down by a large cherry-bark red oak. And lo and behold, in about three minutes, up walk the three gobblers just as boldly as they could march. I had my gun on the old gobbler as he stepped briskly to within thirty yards of the oak. To my great surprise, I simply could not pull the trigger on the old gobbler.

The gobbler which had been shot looked like hell. His head looked as if mud had been splattered on it and he had lost all the sheen of his appearance. I shot the crippled bird instead of the old trophy. The healthy gobblers flew away.

After examining the dead bird, I concluded that he really deserved to be sent to the great clover field in the sky. Several of the shot wounds in the middle of his back, incredibly, had colonies of live maggots in them. The gobbler had a stench to him that would rankle the strongest of stomachs. He would have surely died a slow and agonizing death. I decided to take him to the man who owned the place. I walked to the man's barn, found a grass sack, returned to the hill and placed the turkey in the sack. I then located the man who owned the property.

The property owner was quite appreciative of what I had done and said that he had felt badly all week about messing the turkey up. The turkeys, unknown to me, always roosted close to the edge of the pasture where the man had shot the turkey. After seeing the turkeys again following the shooting, he knew the gobbler was badly wounded. He had even considered taking a rifle and putting the gobbler to sleep, but was afraid the game warden might find him hunting turkeys with an illegal gun. The reason this man's name does not appear in this account is that he asked me not to print his name within the context of this true story. He feels badly, even twenty years later, about taking a bad shot at a gobbler.

I didn't feel too badly, because the man told me to go ahead and hunt all I wanted. I did exactly that and the turkey with the beret on his head got a load of sixes in his head a few short mornings later. He put on a gobbling and strutting extravaganza about a half mile from the hill top.

Midday hunting is not traditionally a proper time to hunt. The only time I go hunting in the middle of the day is after that blood lust has built up so that I feel like I need to kill a gobbler in the worst way. Turkeys are simply too easy to kill during the middle of the day and will boldly approach a caller to be shot.

If you want to hunt during the middle of the day, you must work hard at not breaking a sweat. If you are sweating, then you are moving too fast. Just ease along and you will be surprised at how much ground you can cover by moving ever so slowly.

Each time you approach a likely looking place, sit and call for a while. Be ready to shoot and keep a sharp lookout whether you get a reply from the birds or not. If a turkey doesn't answer, that doesn't mean he isn't on the way, and if a turkey does answer you at this ridiculous time of the day, it won't be long before the bird arrives on the scene. Having called in more than one hundred gobblers during the midday hours, I can tell you that the turkey which answers at this time will often be there very shortly.

You might note that the midday haunts of gobblers are sometimes a long way from their roosting, feeding, and morning strutting zones.

If you are using the middle of the day for scouting, don't assume that turkeys will be close by at daylight. They likely will not be where you encounter them during the middle of the day.

Expect to find turkeys where the temperature is a few degrees cooler. When the warm springtime sunshine hits that feathered coat of the turkey, he gets heated up in a hurry, especially with all that gobbling and strutting. On hot days look for them to have their wings slightly spread and their mouths ajar while cooling off in beech hollows and the like where they can see a considerable distance. They will often be close to a source of water which has shade around it.

Gobblers are still interested in company at this time, but don't think you can call them out on the hot pine ridges where conditions are hot and muggy. Somehow you must get in there where they are. You will spook them if you aren't careful. That's why I don't call too much until I have actually located gobblers.

And Mr. Hopkins' advice on the afternoon eyesight of the gobbler is one hundred percent correct. You do need to be more thoroughly hidden during the late part of the day, since a gobbler does seem to be able to see even better than during the early morning hours.

The moral of this story is that I did the right thing by eliminating the crippled gobbler. I have found that the more right things one does for a turkey, the more one will be rewarded.

* * * * *

Miscellaneous Facts/Opinions

Turkey gobblers are polygamous. They will breed any hen which shows the proper response to the gobbler's mating advances. Wild turkeys, as with most birds, instinctively know how to mate through the process of "sign stimulus". The innate or instinctive reactions to recognized visual signs causes the birds to respond in the proper manner. I.e., the strutting of a gobbler stimulates a hen to crouch, the crouched hen further stimulates the gobbler to mount the hen.

* * * * *

"A Close Call"

5 The Green Dragon Gobbler

There was a time when I could remember just about all the big gobblers which I had encountered. When my mother was living, she would help me keep up with them and my notes served to refresh my memory quite effectively. Gee, even the scores of them which I called for other hunters seemed to make indelible impressions upon my mind, and I could talk for hours upon hours about the gobbler hunts of a single season. The birds which got away were just as crystal clear in my memory as the dead trophies which found their way to the dinner tables of different people.

Maybe it is the numbers of them which have piled up, maybe it's the passing of time, or perhaps the repetition of it all causes the memory to be a little less sharp in dealing with experiences. Whatever the reason, the wild turkey gobblers of these days have to be somewhat special in order for them to register fully. Note taking has become a real necessity and not a luxury. Of course the tough gobblers (and many of them are) still jog our memory quite enough to leave clear prints across our list of experiences.

The more senses one uses during a learning experience, the more likely one is to retain the details of the experience within the catacombs of one's mind. The Green Dragon Gobbler was such an experience that demanded the use of all my senses. He was one of the toughest gobblers I ever hunted. Perhaps that is why I will never forget him as long as I live.

Of course you know that only turkeys which have gained a lofty status within the eyes of hunters are honored with a name—a handle which usually describes some facet of the turkey's being. The name applied may be the result of some peculiar habit of the turkey, a name may be given to a turkey because of the hunter who pursues him the most vigorously, or a name may appear on account of how a turkey's physical appearance strikes one hunter or another. Quite often too, the named turkey gets his place among the elite as a result of all three of the foregoing methods of sticking a name on a wild creature. Then there can be name giving on the basis of the turkey's favorite area of hanging out. Such was the case of the Green Dragon Gobbler.

This bird gave me the slip on numerous occasions in a five acre patch of green dragon plants. The green dragon is a light green herbaceous plant coming from a bulb found in soft swampy places along the flood plains of small creeks within this region of Louisiana. It is a species which is very closely related to the Jack-in-the-Pulpit plant. In this part of the world, they are about twenty inches high during the spring turkey season and among them (because of where they grow) may be found numerous animal food delicacies of the wild turkey. A species of red colored crawfish grows abundantly here and crawls out of the clear running creeks to seek out the green dragon bogs. Gobblers are especially fond of feeding in these areas during the hot mid-morning periods of spring.

The green dragon areas are nearly always eight to ten degrees cooler than other parts of the terrain. Not many other animals of the warm blooded nature hang out there because of the abundant populations of mosquitos which will be found in such forbidding places. For some reason, mosquitos do not bother some old gobblers at all.

I had known about the Green Dragon Gobbler for two years when I took Glen Whetstone from Woodville, Mississippi into his domain. The gobbler had been spared by me for those two years as I was just beginning to get into the practice of "growing trophy gobblers". I had the habit of letting some nice gobblers go just so I could see if they would get wiser as time passed. The Green Dragon Gobbler got incredibly wise—to say the least.

On the morning that I took the Mississippian after the Green Dragon, I witnessed the gobbler make the last mistake that he would make for three years. When we got after the turkey, he had grown into a full bodied long bearded beauty. At four years of age, the bird had long curved spurs.

My friend and I approached the gobbler's roosting area cautiously at daylight. As was the customary practice of this special bird, the turkey gobbled only once on the roost. The gobbler was on the other side of a deep ravine from us, and we made a long loop through the woods to get across the barrier which separated us from the turkey. We hid in a pine thicket about one hundred and fifty yards from where the bird had flown down.

After much calling and waiting, the turkey answered us reluctantly, and was joined in answer by a young gobbler. I leaned over to my hunting partner and informed him that a young bird was down there too, just in case he hadn't realized it. The Mississippi Man nodded, and I sat still again.

Shortly the pair of gobblers began to make their way to us, the young gobbler and the big tom both stopping periodically to strut. No more gobbling was heard. I saw them both duck under a fence about sixty yards from us and stretch their necks to look things over on our side of the wire. Then they stalked us.

The little pine at my back was scarcely what would be considered good hiding cover, and I could not even blink. I had resolved that my friend would have to do the shooting as is preferred anyway when one takes a friend hunting. He had gotten himself ready as good hunters will do and in spite of having to hold his gun up for about three minutes, had the drop on the turkeys completely. It was simply a matter of pulling the trigger. And pull the trigger he did. He could only identify one gobbler head in the thicket and shot the jake just as dead as a fence post. I watched dumbfounded as the big gobbler flew away.

I was a little disappointed, to say the least, at the time of the shooting, because I wanted us to get the long bearded tom. Soon though, I realized that the incident had put the final touches on the production of a real adversary. The old gobbler became super slick after the jake shooting, and as it is often the case, the tragedy of the jake shooting turned into a blessing in disguise.

To say that I had many enjoyable mornings with the bird after that would be a gross understatement. I can say that the Green Dragon Gobbler was the most challenging and enjoyable non-gobbling turkey that I ever dealt with.

Yes, he became a nonparticipating type of bird. He did not gobble more than a dozen times, that I heard, over the next three seasons. He didn't really need to gobble very much. The gobbler developed a loud drumming noise which I could hear clearly at a distance of two hundred yards. He was something special to hear on those crisp spring mornings.

His particular habit was to gobble (maybe) once on the roost while it was still dark on the ground, sail to Mother Earth in an open glade, and parade around with his pet hens until it was time to go to the green dragon patch sometime during the mid-morning hours. Once he gained the green dragon patch, he would boldly approach my calling to within fifty yards, whereupon he would peek-a-boo me all the rest of the day within the confines of the green dragons. He would run his warty head up in a periscope fashion from seemingly everywhere at once and would invariably spot me no matter how well the hiding place seemed to be at the time. I did have the good sense to use only one caller at a time on him and he continued to sneak up on me for years.

He would not answer calling except by drumming loudly and clearly. I never went to the green dragon patch one single time in three years during the spring season when I did not find him there. To say that he had a *quiet reclusive* personality would dub him most correctly.

I still do not understand how he could move through the green dragon thicket so quietly and without making the plants move at least a little bit. A raccoon passing through the plants could be detected by the swaying of the plants all along the coon's course of travel. For three years all I ever saw was the white crown patch on top of the bird's head and just every once in a while, a little bit of his red caruncle. The gobbler never made a single plant move that I could see. He was what one might define as "fluid" among the green dragons.

The herons which hung out in the green dragons did not help matters at all. They would detect me slipping around in the ooze if I attempted to sneak into the middle of the plant bog. Yeah, I even tried sliming around on my belly out there with the bird. One day, as I sneaked over a small rise while squirming on my stomach, a six foot long rattlesnake tried desperately to bite me in the face. That broke up the act.

One might ask at this point, how a fellow could enjoy hunting such a turkey? I mean, it's not every gobbler which joins forces with snakes to do a person in. Not one trip in a hundred do I see a snake while hunting. It seemed as though the snakes and critters were always around the gobbler, and the mosquitos, which never bother me, attacked me in great hordes.

Well, I think it was that incredibly loud drumming noise which thrilled me so. Truly one had to hear it to believe it.

After those numerous encounters over the span of three years, all completely fruitless with respect to actually collecting the bird, a great temptation to give the gobbler to another hunter began to slip in and out of my mind. I decided to try the turkey one more time.

A mile walk from my dad's house brought me to the area where I wanted to listen on this fourth day of the turkey season. It was a rather warm morning, unseasonably so, in fact. No owls were hooting in the gray light and I didn't anticipate hearing any birds gobbling. But one gobbler was really cutting up about half a mile north of where I was standing. This turkey gobbled like a one man gobbling show. He must have sounded off nearly a hundred times before it was yet good light. I figured he must have been secondary in rank to the Green Dragon Gobbler since he was doing so much gobbling on the roost, and as was later discovered, did no gobbling once he hit the ground. He did sound like a good one.

Under ordinary circumstances, I would have stepped up there after him, but I had more serious business at hand. The Green Dragon Gobbler had made a track in the little creek bed the day before. I knew he must have been close to the spot where I was waiting for him to give an indication of his exact location. No word came.

I hid myself as though I knew precisely where he were and pulled out a mouth yelper, the tenth different caller I had tried with the bird. The turkey to the north quit gobbling soon after I had completed a couple of series of yelps. I wondered why he had shut up. Probably had found his hens.

The drumming sound hit me like a bucket of cold water. More careful listening revealed that the sound was coming from my left, and I strained my surveillance in that direction. A tiny motion turned out to be a little warbler. The drumming sounds became fainter. I knew from previous experience that the Green Dragon had gone over the hill with his hens and would soon cross the creek to their feeding grounds among some oak ridges which paralleled the creek. I forced myself to wait a full half hour before beginning to take the circular path I had taken many times before. My route would take me across the creek and between the feeding group of birds and the patch of green dragons where the old gobbler would surely go before morning became noon.

In plenty of time, I was in the new position on the bank overlooking the flood plain where the green dragon plants grew. A very short wait was all that was necessary.

The hens were clearly visible to me as they fed and scratched their way down the hardwood finger. My mouth yelper had never sounded better (to me) and the flat monotoned conversational yelps I imitated brought a couple of yelping responses from the hens. After a while I caught a glimpse of the gobbler which had led me around like a bull with a ring in his nose for three years. His big fan could be seen as a big round outline through the woods which were greening up at an accelerated rate. I lost sight of him very soon and my worst fears were confirmed a short while later.

The troupe of hens with the gobbler following had slipped past me and had entered the area of sliming ooze among those plants. The hens continued to answer me from time to time, but eventually even they became quiet. I knew they were in the bog, but seeing them was impossible. Only the herons were apparent as they jumped from stalk to stalk out in the muddy place. No sign of the turkeys and once again I was mystified at how turkeys could hide so durned effectively in such thin cover and without even trying.

Suddenly the powerful sound of the gobbler was heard again—it had become increasingly hard for me to tell where the bird was since the drumming sound was so loud and strong. The sound seemed to be originating from several directions. The ground almost seemed to vibrate with the subsonic power being emitted by my unseen quarry.

The white top of his head appeared about fifty yards in the plants, as predicted, contrasting sharply with the gulf color of the wave of green dragon plants. I could barely recognize the edge of his eye as the wise bird surveyed the situation. The tip of his rounded fan could be seen briefly and the drumming sound "Vvrrrrooooomph" was heard while the turkey was visible. The sound did not seem to come from where the turkey was standing. "Pffft! Vroooommmph" again. And soon he disappeared as in a wisp of fog or something. I relaxed, because from a multitude of past experiences, I knew that it would be a pretty good while before I heard or saw him again. That is, if he hadn't spotted me already.

I hunkered down and turned to look in another direction. After another half hour, while watching closely, I spotted a hen slipping out through the area I had under scrutiny. I felt pretty good about being able to predict where the group of turkeys was headed. I felt lousy about not being able to do anything about the gobbler with the group. My mind wandered. How could I get next to him? He seemed to anticipate my every move and continuously was out of range of the biggest gun

I could borrow. Fifty yards is entirely too far to shoot at any turkey.

There had been a dozen or so occasions when several of his hens were clearly in range, but not once in three years had the gobbler shown himself for more than a few seconds at a time. And those appearances had been at ranges greater than is expected of any shotgun.

I had used all the calls and callers I knew of. I had also waited in ambush, a stunt which I do not like to admit to having done. I had called from every place one could imagine. The numerous little craters all along the ridges were holes created from my butt being parked there for such long periods of time. I know I must have heard the turkey drumming and strutting on at least a hundred occasions—usually a pretty good indication that one might be getting close to getting a shot at a gobbler. I was beginning to think the turkey might be a supernatural being. He had that mystique about him.

The drumming sound, not movement, brought me out of my daydream of past experiences. The white crown patch appeared again just at the top of the plants and the calculated distance was again fifty yards. Of course the gobbler kept on traveling; I think the bird had spotted me. Little did I know that the game bird would be dead within one hour of these passing thoughts.

When I last saw the little entourage moving from left to right, I knew there were two hens and the gobbler. Or at least I thought there were two hens. It appeared that a hen was leading the gobbler and another hen was bringing up the rear. The second hen was not a turkey.

Suddenly there was a loud commotion of Plips! and Cutts! and flying up cackles as a half dozen turkeys became airborne. No fewer than three hens alighted right over my head, and the gobbler flew up about forty yards from me and perched in the fork of a beech tree. As I watched, a couple of his tail feathers came drifting down to the ground. Some unseen attacker had very nearly put an end to the career of the gobbler.

Sure enough, within minutes, a large bobcat came skulking out of the bog, leaping up on a log next to the creek. The cat glared over his shoulder at the gobbler in the tree and was gone as quietly and quickly as he had appeared. The old gobbler was locked onto the presence of the cat and moved his head in a circular pattern following the cat's progress through the swamp.

I thought about shooting the gobbler right then and there, but I really didn't have a good shot. I just watched and sat stone still. If you have ever tried to sit motionless for any length of time, you know how I felt after a full hour.

It was a good thing I didn't shoot, because after that hour of trying to look like a stump, the turkeys all flew straight down to the ground. The gobbler sailed over to meet with the hens a scant twenty feet from me. I was puzzled greatly at how they had silently decided without a vote about the correct moment to fly down. The exact period of waiting for the cat to leave seemed to be somehow by mutual agreement.

Those of you who have patted me on the back for my sporting practices with wild turkeys, please forgive me for what I have to report. The Green Dragon Gobbler died of shotgun wounds suffered about the head and neck following a near fatal encounter with a bobcat. I killed with passion and did not lose a wink of sleep about having shot the bird when he landed out of those durn green dragon plants. In the open woods, he looked like a real turkey, and a hell of a good one at that. His eleven inch beard is among my favorites and the memory of the long hard hunt will forever be one of my finest recollections.

* * * * *

Miscellaneous Facts/Opinions

Gobbling is not part of the sign stimulus apparatus within a flock of turkeys.

The gobbling of male turkeys is clearly a display of territorial behavior. Like the song bird which sings in the spring, the male turkey sounds off to make his presence and therefore his territory known to all potential rivals of his species.

The out stretched neck held parallel to the ground is the threatening posture for male turkeys.

Color changes may occur within a matter of seconds in the head region of a male turkey indicating the mood of the bird.

* * * * *

"Glen Whetstone and trophy"

"He had a long tail and was streamlined. . . .
His breast sponge was small and hung low"

6 The Circuit Rider

The state of Mississippi is just full of good country folks. The magnolia state is also blessed with some of the finest turkey habitat to be found anywhere. I have done quite a bit of visiting and quite a bit of turkey hunting up there. I have done some hunting with friends and relatives, but usually, I just pick a spot on the map in one of the many national forest areas. There are over a million acres of national forest lands scattered throughout Mississippi. Much of it is within an hour's drive of my house.

Sometimes, I even get a tip about the whereabouts of a gobbler from folks who know that I like to get after the big bird. Such was the case four years ago.

My wife and I have coached basketball at the academy in Gloster for four years. It was during the winter of 1982 that I got a hot tip from one of our players.

We were traveling to one of those far away road games. This one player, named Smokey Petty, seemed to be having some problems in the back of the bus. He wasn't a bad boy; it was just that the cheerleaders caused him to be, er well, a little bit "off". I invited Smokey to join me in the front of the bus for the remainder of the long ride. That must have been pure torture for Smokey because he wiggled and squirmed like a cat in a room full of rocking chairs. We had about two more hours of riding to do, so we gave Smokey a chart to ponder concerning his shooting statistics from our recent games. That kept him quiet and still for a little while.

After about thirty minutes of riding with me in the front of the bus, Smokey had devised an escape plan. He began by distracting me with a ridiculous lie about seeing a big buck on the side of the highway. The whole bus swayed to one side as the load of kids (and me too) rushed to that side of the bus to get a look at the buck. Of course there was no buck to be seen. I scolded old Smokey about such tomfoolery. It took about five minutes to get everyone settled again.

This did get Smokey into a conversation with me about hunting. He was a smart boy and a likeable fellow too. I found it very hard to ride him too hard. And yes, I did ask him if he liked to hunt turkeys. Smokey said he didn't mess with turkeys because it interfered with his baseball, but that he did know where a whole gang of them were. He claimed to see about forty in a flock every morning on his way to school. Smokey even went so far as to point out that no one ever hunted up there near his house. I knew that Smokey lived near some two hundred thousand (200,000) acres of national forest and that he just might, for once, be telling the truth.

Finally, Smokey sprung the deal on me. He told me that he would be a good little boy (he was a senior) and that he would show me exactly where the turkeys were if only I would let him return to the back of the bus with the other kids.

After mulling it over for a while, I took out a piece of paper and wrote down what we agreed. The boy rode to and from all the remaining games while perched like a little monkey in the back of the bus. The cheerleaders rode in the front with me, but true to our written agreement, Smokey was allowed to ride in the back.

Every week or so, it was necessary to remind Smokey about such things as "A Man's Word", being honest, and growing up, and so forth. I was real pleased with his progress. That young man could run and jump and shoot that basketball. We had Smokey and some of his teammates down to our place for a deer hunt. Smokey could shoot hoops better than deer; he missed a good buck.

We did have a good basketball season and it was over all too soon. The only good thing about the end of basketball season is the fact that turkey season is not too far away by then.

About a week before the spring turkey season opened, I rode to Gloster to check on Smokey. He was practicing baseball and could not go with me to scout for turkeys. He did live up to his part of the bargain by placing an "X" on a topo map where the turkeys were supposed to be.

I left for the "Forest". When I arrived at the place where the turkeys were reported to be in great numbers, I had trouble finding a parking place. There were trucks and campers everywhere and I saw license plates from half the states in the country. I got out of there and didn't even think about that place again until the turkey season was half over.

I thumped several longbeards at home and had collected a trophy on a private place in Mississippi. One day, just as an afterthought, I swung by the place Smokey had pointed out.

There were no people in evidence for miles; no trucks, no campers, no hunters. I decided to make a mid morning scouting hike. I found out what the attraction was with all the hunters.

Turkeys! And lots of them. Turkey sign was all over the woods. The numerous little creeks all had gobbler tracks on the little sand spits, and the beech ridges were really scratched up. A forty acre clear cut had about fifty dusting holes in and around it. Huge park like timber stands were the key term here. I'll bet there was twenty thousand board feet of timber per acre for ten square miles. It was a paradise!

As usual for that part of the country, turkeys responded well to my calling. In less than an hour, I had called up and bagged a big gobbler with a ten inch beard and inch long spurs.

At the sound of my shot, a very shrill gobble echoed back to me from somewhere over in the middle of that six thousand acre block of heavy timber. That was the first that I heard of the turkey which was to drive me crazy for two weeks. The remainder of the season was going to belong to this *circuit riding* gobbler which I came to know personally as a test to my will and hunting skill. I was to have some good luck after a long run of bad luck with him.

I presented the turkey I had bagged to a lady in Crosby, and drove home. Now what I needed was an excuse to spend a little more time up there in "Smokey's Woods".

I still had one turkey left to fill out my limit and I wanted another longbeard, something exceptional was all that I would accept. I just knew the turkey which had gobbled at my shot must have been a really good one. His gobble was long and every note was separated from the one preceeding it. I heard each of the individual notes plainly, even at the great distance following the echo from my shot.

One of the landowners I work for as a timber consultant owned a good bit of timber land in and around that part of Mississippi. I approached him with the proposition of checking out all of his land in that area for pine beetles. He said by all means for me to get in there and make sure the bugs were not on his property. I did exactly that. For two weeks, I hunted the gobbler early and late. The remainder of the time was spent checking timber stands for pine beetles. I didn't find an unusual amount of beetle activity, but that old gobbler on the national forest certainly was active. Here's what the old rascal did to me.

The first morning, the turkey did not gobble at all until around seven o'clock, some two hours after flying down time. I had heard several cars and trucks on the numerous little gravel roads at daylight. There had also been some strange sounding owl hooting going on.

I deduced that these turkeys must have been wise to a lot of owl hooting. I just remained in position and waited for all the riding up and down on the roads to cease.

Everything got just as still and peaceful very soon after the traffic thinned out. I did no calling during my two hour wait while I was sitting in a good place to hear a turkey gobble. I was located about one quarter of a mile from a little creek and within hearing of a forty acre clear cut. Gee, I knew from all the visible signs that the turkeys were indeed present and there seemed to be no sense in spooking them even more by walking around too much.

Many times, in areas such as this, the boss gobbler will be the first one to sound off. And if the boss gobbler does not sound off in the morning, the other turkeys may not gobble either. This is not always the case, but often happens to be true.

The old gobbler finally did gobble. He was way beyond the clear cut, probably over half a mile from me. Those open pine ridges always make for good hearing range. When he gobbled the second time, I got a good fix on his location and lit out in his direction, traveling from east to west. He continued gobbling, but seemed to be the same distance from me even after I had walked a quarter of a mile. I had crossed two gravel roads traveling in the direction of the gobbling turkey when I realized the turkey was heading across the country. I heard him gobble until around ten o'clock and never did get close to him.

Upon giving up the chase for the day, I found that a three mile walk was involved in getting back to the truck. A careful study of the topo map took place back at the truck. I had really walked a long ways, but so had the gobbler. I drove the truck around to where I could get close to the area where I had lost contact with the gobbler. This was a classic circuit rider apparently.

Another check of the map revealed another series of little creeks to the west. I drove around there and found another clear cut. That clear cut was the place to be the next morning. I spent the rest of the day checking for pine beetles.

Riding around in the national forest with all those little roads running in every direction can be confusing. I got lost the next morning before daylight, and wound up on some little road which wasn't even on the map. Since I was still in the middle of Forest Service land, I pulled over and waited for daylight.

Several gobblers began to sound off less than two hundred yards from where I was parked. They were definitely not the turkey I was looking for, but I walked out in the woods and played with them a little while anyway. The pair of gobblers came up to within thirty yards of my hiding place and it was easy to see that they were pretty gobblers, but not likely as good as the one I had been chasing. I told the pair of gobblers how stupid they were. Turkeys can really get a move on when they get scared.

It was a long day checking for pine beetles, but just before dark, I had found my way back to the second clear cut area. I imitated the fly-up cackle and two gobblers answered me from the little bottoms beyond the clear cut. Neither of them was the one I was after. Back to square one.

A couple of days passed before I returned to the original haunts of the shrill sounding gobbler. A disgustingly windy morning was on hand and rain was in the forecast. No birds gobbled and I walked the long miles over to the second clear cut and became intimately familiar with the area.

I did no calling during the morning.

Some serious gravel road driving of my own took place later in the day. I began to see how to proceed from one place to another with a minimum of effort. There were no hunters out on this particular day and I figured they must have all given up. I was wrong in that supposition.

I became fired up that night when the afternoon storm and ensuing rain stopped at around ten p.m.

I began my fourth morning of hunting the circuit rider. It had been a while since I had heard him gobble, several days in fact. At daylight, the trucks were patrolling the roads again. It was a beautiful morning; the rain had cooled things off considerably, and no wind was blowing.

Strangely, a two year old bird was answering some man's imitation of the barred owl. I was really puzzled by this. Why did the younger turkey gobble? Maybe the circuit rider wasn't home. I jumped in my truck and drove the three miles over to the second clear cut. No sooner had I got out of the truck than I heard the one I was after cut loose right out in the middle of the clear cut. What a fine duel we were to have on that morning!

On two different set ups, I had him walking the line out there, walking back and forth and gobbling. Both times though, he gave me that, "I'll see you later", gobble and continued his trek eastward toward the first clear cut. Again at around ten o'clock I lost contact with the bird, but I had learned a great deal about him. He especially liked cackling and would answer a hawk call nearly every time. He must have gobbled over a hundred times during the morning.

I felt good after being so decidely bested by the turkey. After all, I had a gravel road entry at each end of his circuit. All that was necessary now was to find out which end he was roosting on, and go wait for him at the other end of his circuit. This, apparently, was the type of circuit rider which made his whole circuit on a daily basis. That became my game plan, to wait for him at the other end. All this walking after a vagabond gobbler, plus all the miles I had to walk looking at timber, was going to do me in.

Now I knew that he must have been near the first clear cut for the next morning. So, all I had to do was get to the second clear cut before mid morning and surely the old turkey would show up.

I slept late the next morning and did not arrive at my planned destination until eight-thirty. I proceeded to a spot where the turkey had walked the line on me the day before. I set up in plenty of time, and even though I heard no gobbling, I knew my bird was on the way.

At a little after nine o'clock, some pilgrim came walking down through the woods squawking with a box caller. Boy, this was just a little bit frustrating! There is a humorous side to everything though. The fellow with the box was quite a show. He had the box caller in his coat, and all kinds of racket squawked out his coat with every few steps that he took. I believe the guy must have been hard of hearing, because every time the box made a noise, the poor pilgrim would stop and listen carefully for long moments. After a few more steps, the box would squawk again, and the man would stop again and listen some more. The hunter finally sat down by a pine tree about one hundred yards from me. I just sat there and watched and dared not move. The pilgrim appeared to be asleep. I know he was very still, because the box made no more racket.

A while later, the old gobbler announced his arrival on the same ridge the hunter was situated on. The guy immediately sprang to his feet and raced off down through the woods, but in the opposite direction of where the turkey had gobbled. The man and the box caller ran out of hearing. I just sat still.

The turkey finally gobbled again, he had gone on past where I was sitting, so I got up and moved closer to him. After calling a couple of times and getting no answer, I slipped back to where I was to begin with. I sat still without calling for about thirty minutes.

Shortly, the old gobbler appeared on the pine knoll where the man had been sitting. The tom strutted up and down over there. He would not answer any of the soft calls I was now giving him, but would strut up a storm with every call. The gobbler stayed puffed up in a big ball until he heard that box caller off in the distance. The bird looked long and hard, then walked off towards a little creek away from the sound of the box caller. He was a dandy gobbler and I knew he had some age on him. When not strutting, his breast sponge seemed to be formed like a tight ball which hung low on his breast. His tail feathers looked longer than is normal too. These are pretty good indicators of old age while observing a gobbler in the field.

When I got back to the truck, there sat the pilgrim with the box caller. He had the tail gate of his pickup down and was sitting there eating something called "blood boudin", a concoction of Cajun origin. I soon learned that the character was from New Orleans. He had seen my truck and figured there must have been, as he put it, "a hot turkey around". He had not killed any turkeys, but said that he had been having a ball. In fact, he had never killed a gobbler in his life. He had been hunting for six years. Finally, the guy asked me if I had seen anything or heard something. I told him there was a gobbler in there all right. I didn't tell him the turkey had walked right up on that pine knoll where he had been sitting.

The novice hunter seemed to be a little bit skeptical when I told him there were two gobblers in a hollow right next to the road a couple of miles from where we were. I offered to show him where they were. He kind of looked at me funny and said, "Really!?" The poor fellow followed me down the road and I sicked him on the two younger gobblers I had fooled with before. I figured that would keep him busy for several days.

I found a pine beetle colony that afternoon which kept me busy for several days. It was a beautiful morning when I got back up in the forest after the old circuit rider again. The morning traffic was out again and everything around the clear cut to the west was profoundly quiet. The plan was to just sit until the old one came along later, or sounded off close by. At seven o'clock I heard a shot way down the road and as was his habit, the old gobbler answered the echo from the shot. He was on a beech ridge overlooking a little spring creek.

He answered my cackling when I got close to him, but moved away. I followed. He gobbled again a little further out. I ran way around him—I thought. I had not gone far enough and his next answer to the hawk call had me up and away again, running in a big circle through hills and hollows. I set up to call him again.

My breath had just returned when the rascal gobbled again. He was off to the south; he had taken another drainage system. He must have been three hundred yards from where I sat. I gobbled at him; he gobbled back. A lonesome hen yelp imitation got another gobble out of him, but it was that, "I'll see you later", type of gobble.

Paralleling the ridges he was in, I took off in a fast trot. Pretty soon I found myself three miles from the truck and looking at the other clear cut. I didn't hear anymore from him that day. He was indeed a tough bird. More than I had expected, this turkey knew the ropes of this game we were playing.

Later that day, I ran into the pilgrim from New Orleans at a country store belonging to the Foreman family in Crosby. In the back of his truck was a nice gobbler with a nine inch beard. The very irridescent bird looked like a very big two year old gobbler. The hunter told me that the turkeys had been right where I put him and that he couldn't thank me enough. He even offered me some of that blood boudin. I refused politely.

The story of his hunt was incredible. The gobbler had walked out in a log road at the same time the hunter had appeared in the road. With no where to go or hide, the man had just crouched right in the road. With the gobbler in plain sight, he had taken out his caller and made some yelps. The turkey walked away from him down the road, not running, but walking fast in the opposite direction. The man followed and when he rounded a bend in the tote road, there stood the gobbler less than twenty five yards away. Shortly, a flopping turkey was losing feathers in the road. "One shot right in the head", bragged the pilgrim. Man, I'll tell you that turkey hunting is a strange game. Some days the danged things just commit suicide.

I got a late start the next morning. When I arrived at the second clear cut, the old gobbler was out in the middle of it gobbling his head off. There just had to be a way to get up on this old rascal. I decided to just follow along behind him that day. I called and he moved away gobbling, heading toward the other clear cut some three miles away.

I did no running through the woods on this day. The turkey and I had a pitched battle going all morning. Again he walked the line on me a couple of times and again he left for the other end of his circuit. I was very familiar with his country by now, and on this fine April morning, I stopped a good distance short of the clear cut. It was mid morning.

The old rascal was between me and the clear cut. When he gave me that "come on with me" gobble as he headed out in the clear cut, I did not answer him. I sat down there in a beech and magnolia park and listened to the gobbler raise all kinds of hell up there in the clear cut. He had walked three miles dragging me along and was still full of energy. I finally eased up to the edge of the clear cut and climbed a gum tree.

He was out there all right. I looked at him strutting around two hens for about thirty minutes. Every once in a while, the gobbler would break strut and gobble in four directions to all points of the compass, turning first one way and then another. Soon another hen joined the trio and the turkey ceased his gobbling for the day.

The sun got hot out there and the turkeys left the clear cut. By inching along inside the woodline, I made my way to the point where the group of turkeys had entered the woods. An assembly yelp imitation got no response, but in a few minutes, I began to hear drumming. A different gobbler walked up. He had a much shorter beard than the old boy I was after. This gobbler walked out in the clear cut and began dusting under a lone tree in the clearing.

All was quiet for another half hour and then I could hear the drumming again. I made some real soft sounds and the drumming got louder. I got a tiny glimpse of my turkey. He was not in a presentable position to be shot. He didn't hang around long and I soon lost all contact with him, both by sight and sound. That wrapped it up for the day. I had only three days of season left. Having a good time with a gobbler is fun all right, but I really did want to bag this bird.

The next morning I got an early start. It was on a Friday and for some reason, there was no morning traffic with owl hooting going on. The old gobbler cut loose right at daylight less than one half mile from where I had last seen him. I started a calm walk towards the turkey. About five or six other turkeys got cranked up along the way. It was a pretty morning and the dew was on the ground even in the big timber. The gobbler had flown down when I reached him and I did not call, just followed him along. On this morning, the turkey was gobbling on his own as he made his eastward trek.

Some two hours after he had flown down, both the turkey and I were on the same long ridge, him on the east and me on the west end. Now was the time to try him with the callers. I pulled out the Morgan Caller and gave a soft cackle. He answered down there about one hundred and fifty yards. Immediately, I dropped off to one side of the ridge to get out of the sun which was in my eyes. I suspected that something was going to happen and I most certainly didn't want to get caught up on the top of that ridge.

A long period of silence followed. I concentrated completely on not getting restless; I did not move a bit. My gun was trained on top of the ridge.

Suddenly he gobbled again about seventy five yards down the ridge. He was over the hump of a little rise on my side of the hill. An ID cluck and a soft purr with my slate caller failed to bring any response. A few minutes passed and I heard the drumming sound. Then I could see his old warty head sticking up over the brow of the ridge about thirty yards away. I looked long and hard, with my gun on him the whole time. I couldn't be sure if he was the right one. I didn't want to shoot that lesser gobbler that I had seen dusting in the clear cut.

Finally, the gobbler took a few steps forward and I knew that he was the right one. While he was standing erect, partially obscured by a couple of bushes, he made the "Vrroooooom" sound again. Then he went into his snake like approach and literally vanished into thin air. I knew he was coming straight at me, and I lowered my gun barrel so I could see any telltale signs better. The bead was not exactly on him when his head popped up a scant ten yards away. I corrected the inch of difference and shot at the same time. The ordeal was over.

I don't think I have ever killed a more beautiful specimen. He was about seventeen pounds in weight, had a very small breast sponge, and he had an eleven inch beard that was pencil thin. His spurs were one and one fourth inches long and were very curved and needle sharp. I was a happy hunter.

I must say that the bird did exactly what I expected him to do. In fact, the circuit riding type of gobbler may patrol areas even larger than this one did. If you want to kill one, you might employ three sporting tactics. You can circle ahead of him, you can follow behind him, or you can wait for him at one end of his circuit.

Some vagabonds don't visit all parts of their route on the same day. In some cases, circuit riders may be gone for a couple of days at a time, sometimes as long as a week. Finding them at home can be a serious problem. I have had more success dealing with them by staying in contact with them every day until they goof up. You must be careful and not spook the bird or he will really become difficult.

Anyway you approach these sultans of the circuit, it is likely to require several days to get the drop on one of them. And the circuit rider is not always a handsome boss gobbler like the one I killed in "Smokey's Woods". Two year old gobblers are frequently vagabond in nature. You can tell them from the older vagabonds by the sound of their gobbles.

Usually a vagabond gobbler will announce his arrival at each stopping point, especially if he is one of those gobblers which I call a preferred male.

The thing which makes the vagabond gobbler so tough if he is a preferred male is the fact that he is accustomed to hens showing up when he arrives in an area. Often quite an entourage will show up to suit his fancy. Most vagabonds don't stay long in the company of hens. When the hens arrive, he struts and puts on his show. If mating occurs, so much the better. If the hens feed off from him, he may just be on his way to the next stop.

They are tough—and usually worth every bit of effort put into the hunting of one of them.

* * * * *

Miscellaneous Facts/Opinions

The drumming sounds of male turkeys are caused by the escape of air from within the turkey. However, no one seems to completely understand the mechanics of this sound.

The oil glands within the pygostyle region (last thing to go through a hole in the fence) of turkeys, both male and female, provide a substance which, when applied to the feathers with the bird's bill insulates the turkey against cold and wet. The gobbler assumes a glossy appearance after he has groomed himself with oil from his pygostyle gland.

The bones of the wild turkey are pneumatic; they have hollow air spaces within them and are reinforced with struts like those found in airplane wings. This engineering makes the wings and boney structure both lightweighted and very strong.

The feathers of a turkey, like those of other birds, are made of a network of hooks and barbs which make each component of the feather adhere to the adjoining one. No wonder the feathers of a big turkey can shed pellets from a shotgun at longer distances.

Feathers are shed in a pattern during the molting process. The once a year molt of turkeys calls for the loss of one feather on each side of the symmetry, so that the bird is not denuded during the process. As the lost feather begins to grow back, another one is molted until the bird has replaced all of its feathers. This phenomenom occurs during the summer months.

* * * * *

"5½ foot Canebrake Rattler"

"Changed Himself into a White House Cat"

7 The Mystery of Little Beaver Creek

My Uncle Percy Rogers once owned four hundred acres on Little Beaver Creek. It was the place where my dad grew up, but no one has lived there since 1934. It was a typical abandoned farm; the ground in the creek bottoms was fertile enough, but the upland portion of the property had some of the poorest soil to be found anywhere in this part of the world.

When I came to know the place it had reverted completely to the wild. All the old farm fields had grown up in pine timber and huckleberry bushes, while the creek bottom itself had become a beautiful stretch of beech and oak stands with a scattering of huge spruce pines. A pipeline intersected the creek right in the middle of the property. Wild game was abundant, complete with a large flock of wild turkeys, which traveled Little Beaver Creek. When springtime came, the pipeline and pine/huckleberry thickets attracted hens for nesting. Lots of grass grew among the huckleberrys and the pipeline was kept neatly manicured by the gas company. It was common to see longbearded gobblers fly down on a large beaver dam which backed up the water for a mile in the creek.

Since the land was not posted for a long time, local folks hunted the property pretty much as they pleased. The people who I knew were pretty good sportsmen and would not shoot a hen turkey for any amount of money. Some considered it a disgrace to kill a young gobbler. In fact, most of that locale had a good population of turkeys in the '60s and '70s. There were lots of gobbling birds everywhere and not just on Uncle Percy's place.

Out of the sporting sort of hunting which took place out there, a legend grew. There came to be known a wild gobbler which hung out in one of the most dense huckleberry thickets you can imagine. He was known as the "The Ghost", "The Invisible Turkey", "Mosseyhead", and a variety of other names not suitable for print. Mr. Julius Kirkland, of Felixville, who was one man who took his turkeys anyway he could get them, said that the gobbler must not have been a corn eater, or he would not have lived so long. Mr. Murray Wilson, of nearby Clinton, La., claimed to have actually got a glimpse of the turkey, describing him as a little old turkey with a long tail. Mr. Ellis Hopkins, who hunted the turkey religiously for a while, said that he felt as if the turkey were a mosseyheaded gobbler even though he had never laid eyes on the bird.

All agreed the gobbler was unkillable. I questioned their veracity at one group session we had, but all the old veteran hunters insisted the turkey was indeed real. The gobbler had been gobbling from the same huckleberry thicket for at least six years. I did not speculate about what he was or how long he had gobbled in some thicket, but did announce that I was going to kill him. I was a sophomore in college at the time and just full of myself.

All the men who hunted the area said they would be glad to let me have him all to myself if I would stay away from a couple of other places where I was known to worry the turkeys pretty regularly. In those days people believed in hunting a turkey one on one. It was a common practice for folks to stay out of another hunter's way. Everyone reciprocated favors of this sort. There were very few secrets about turkeys in those days.

Soon thereafter, Tommy Woodside, a hunting buddy of mine from Jackson, and I rode over to the ghost turkey's hangout to put an end to the legend. I had heard enough about this bird. We took Jack Schaeffer of Lake Providence with us. Jack was armed with the most ominous looking ten gauge shotgun I ever saw, which he gladly demonstrated on tin cans at every opportunity. Several times on the way to the hunting grounds we wondered out loud if we were crazy or not. It was raining cats and dogs, especially cats. Not even the terrific bolts of lightning which smashed around us could dull our enthusiasm though and we continued on our way in the stormy pre-dawn weather.

Shortly before daylight, just as we arrived at our destination, the wind and lightning stopped. In less than ten minutes, the rain had also quit and the stars came out just as pretty as you please. We could not believe our good fortune as we hiked into the woods.

Mr. Wilson had given us exact directions to where the turkey lived and I knew precisely where to go. All I had to do was find a certain post oak on the pipeline and we would be able to hear the turkey gobble from there. We instructed Jack to go a mile further into the woods with that cannon of his. And Jack, with his giraffe-like gait, was soon far ahead of Tom and me as we approached our listening post. It was getting light and we were right on time.

Within minutes of arriving at the post oak hill, a rather weak sounding gobble rose up from the thicket to our east. A little while passed and the birds began to sing. The next gobble was a little stronger and I can assure you that it was very real. The turkey was less than one hundred yards from where we stood. Tom and I quietly slipped into position to call and wait for the gobbler.

Tom situated himself by a tree and looked directly into the thicket of pines and huckleberry bushes. I sat on the opposite side of Tom's tree and watched the pipeline. I settled down and then gave a low series of yelps—no answer. All the birds were now singing and the crows started cutting up. Still no more gobbling was heard. A little while later I did hear something fly down.

We sat motionless for a long time. I was sure all of my body had gone to sleep when I began to hear the familiar drumming sound. I could not tell exactly where it was coming from, but was better advised than to turn my head all around looking for the origin of the drumming. I stared at the pipeline opening hoping the old tom would step out in the opening like so many of them do. My line of vision was partially obscured, but I could see one forty foot section of the pipeline pretty well. The grass was less than six inches tall there. Anything in the pipeline was dead meat since that opening was less than twenty five yards away.

Finally I did catch sight of some movement, a tiny one, down the pipeline. I got my gun up and watched the opening. Something white was coming into my sight lane. To my great surprise, a snow white house cat appeared and walked leisurely down the pipeline, his long tail waving in the air as he returned home from a night of rambling. Nothing else appeared.

A few minutes later, Tom asked me in a whisper why I didn't shoot. When I told him it was a house cat, Tom just shook his head and looked back at the thicket. We remained quiet and still until it was time to go. We did not hear or see anything else.

Jack had walked durn near into Mississippi and while we were waiting for him to come out, Tom and I examined the pipeline for evidence. There was a fresh set of rather smallish gobbler tracks in the pipeline, made since the predawn rain. Tom looked at me quizzically, and I reassured him that the only thing that I saw was a house cat. Tom wanted to know where the house cat tracks were in the soft rain soaked ground. I didn't know.

Tom's questions got on my nerves because I knew quite well that I had seen no gobbler. I had seen a snow white house cat. I was just kidding Tom when I offered that maybe the gobbler had seen me get my gun up. In order to keep from getting shot, the thing had changed himself into the house cat. Tom didn't laugh, but Jack said he thought he would put some silver pellets in his shells before he returned to this land of mystery.

We stopped at the Malt Shop in Clinton on the way home. The crew of turkeys hunters was there. Mr. Wilson informed us that he had been seeing a house cat back there on the pipeline for years, and the cat belonged to Mrs. DeLee who lived about a mile down the road. The cat apparently visited all over the country and could be seen just about anywhere. That made me feel better about the cat, but what about the gobbler tracks in the pipeline?

According to Mr. Wilson, again, it was not uncommon to see the gobbler's tracks in one's own tracks. They all seemed to be thoroughly amused by the state of agitation I had worked myself into. Every hunter in East Feliciana knew about it before dark of that very day. It was told all over how I had actually let this old turkey walk up to within twenty-five yards of where I was sitting and that I couldn't even see him. I became possessed with a terrific passion to kill this gobbler.

I missed twenty-one classes at LSU that spring chasing that gobbler. Some mornings he would gobble three or four times and on other mornings he would not gobble at all. On every single morning that I pursued him, I could hear him drumming all around me. I called from a variety of places and the results were always the same. I even found the tree that he preferred to roost in. It was a small pine less than thirty feet tall and there must have been two gallons of droppings under the tree. I resorted to waiting for him to come to roost at that tree. I never heard or saw him in the afternoons.

One morning I took about eight of my botany lab classmates up there and we surrounded him. No sight or sound from the turkey. No tracks either.

At the end of the season, I was exhausted. It was the worst season I could recall ever having. That didn't bother me so much as the fact that I never even saw the gobbler. I was mentally beaten by the bird and was convinced that I could not kill him. I began to think like the other hunters, announcing the turkey was unkillable.

That summer I met two men with whom I became friends. One was Colonel Bill Hornsey, of Baton Rouge, a well known outdoor writer, who was to have a lasting effect on my ideas about hunting and life in general. The other was Bobby Joe King, a good friend now and part of our present day hunting fraternity.

One day the three of us began a conversation about hunting and, of course, the subject of turkeys came up. I began to tell them about the huckleberry thicket gobbler on Uncle Percy's place. Colonel Hornsey laughed and laughed when I told him what a predicament I had worked myself into with the gobbler. Bobby Joe amused me by claiming that he could kill the gobbler, with no trouble. Bobby Joe had never even seen a wild turkey at that time. I learned though, that BJ was not to be taken lightly, not because he played defensive tackle for the Tigers, but because he turned out to be a talented person in any kind of endeavor.

Colonel Hornsey's mood became serious when I told him I was afraid I might be dismissed from school if I missed classes like that again. The Colonel said that the three of us ought to be sure we bagged the bird on the first day of the season, if that was the case.

The Colonel promised to go with BJ and me up there for a scouting trip in the fall, and he left us with a thought. It seems as though the Colonel believed the turkey was an example of a living thing looking just like his surroundings by perfect camouflage or shading. He said that was often the case when an animal had lived in an area for a long time.

All throughout the fall semester, Bobby Joe kept reminding me about how he was going to kill the gobbler come turkey season. Colonel Hornsey and I did go up there so he could look over the country. We covered the old turkey's thicket like a pair of detectives.

Colonel Hornsey asked me if the place was even thicker in the spring. I told him it was much the same except there was more grass growing under the huckleberry bushes. He said it was easy to imagine a gobbler being so hard to see in such a place.

Seems as though the Colonel thought the only obstacle to killing the gobbler was in seeing the bird. "You'll have to look for his eye. If you get close enough to hear him drumming, then you can find his eye. The turkey's eye is round and he can't hide that," were the words I thought about all winter. I thought this might be a pretty far fetched idea, but I pondered it for a long time.

I scheduled all afternoon classes for the spring semester and a night class too. I was ready for the season. I went and listened from the post oak hill for six straight mornings prior to the opening day and the same little old shrill rattle kept ringing up out of the huckleberries. Bobby Joe went with me on a couple of mornings. He really got fired up about the gobbler. I could tell BJ was just itchin' for me to ask him along, so I told BJ that he could hunt the old gobbler all by himself the first morning if he wanted to. The Colonel had been lecturing me about attitudes of hunters. He claimed the more generous a hunter is in hunting endeavors with other people, the luckier that hunter will become with his own adventures.

On opening day, BJ, the Colonel, and I were up there on Uncle Percy's place. Coloney Hornsey and I walked way back on Little Beaver and left BJ at the gobbler's thicket. We had a fine morning in the woods, the three of us.

The Colonel and I called up a couple of gobblers, but did not take a shot. We just didn't see one that we wanted to kill. At nine o'clock, we began the long hike back down the pipeline to see how BJ had fared with the ghost turkey.

Just as we topped a hill on the pipeline, we saw a big defensive lineman type of fellow disappear into the woods west of the pipeline. The Colonel and I crouched to keep out of sight while we tried to figure out what BJ was up to. It didn't take long, for a few moments later, a black bird a bit larger than a big rooster walked out into the pipeline and gobbled. The turkey left the pipeline following in BJ's steps.

We ducked into the woods and in a hurry closed the distance to within a hundred yards of the action. It was here that the creek bottom gave way to the jungle of huckleberries. I looked carefully now and the whole place was indeed a dark shadowy place, even though it was a bright sunshiny day. The little canopy provided by the green topped bushes made dark spots all throughout the thicket and the layers of dead straw on the ground gave the place a very dank and dungeon-like appearance.

Suddenly BJ appeared in the pipeline again and impressed us with the realistic yelping he was doing. BJ immediately left the pipeline, and the little gobbler was not long in popping out in the opening. It was a funny sight as the hunter and the gobbler repeated this act several times. It reminded me of those cartoons where the character doing the chasing soon becomes the character being chased. I wish I could have laughed about it at the time, but I was too serious about the old mini-gobbler.

After a while BJ came out and just stood there. He glanced at his watch. We got his attention by waving our arms. He trudged up to where we were. BJ was wringing wet and informed us that the gobbler and he had been walking around and around in the thicket since daylight.

We held a quick conference. The Colonel deployed us in a triangle with each of us being one hundred yards apart. We were to take turns calling and were not to move from where we sat down until noon.

Bobby Joe's first yelp brought a quick answer from the little tom. He answered me a few minutes later from less than thirty yards away. I soon heard him drumming up a storm. I looked hard for the turkey, but could not see him. I called again and he responded in the pipeline close to the Colonel, but too far to shoot. Bobby Joe called again and the bird rattled out another answer. Then all was quiet for a long time.

Finally I heard the drumming again. The noise got louder. Then the drumming sounded right next to me. I looked hard without moving my head. I did see the turkey's eye first! He was about fifteen yards out there directly under a huckleberry bush and the whole bird seemed to take shape around that blinking hazel eye.

The turkey didn't see me and began to move to my right. I was impressed with the way he walked. He looked like the black shadows and brown stems of the peeling huckleberry stems. When the bird was just right, I snapped up my shotgun and finished him with a shot to the head. The thing did not even flop!

Everybody was excited, especially me. The turkey weighed an even twelve pounds, had a thin nine inch beard and did not have any spurs at all. He had a row of feathers growing up the back of his head like a hen turkey, but had the red caruncles of a gobbler, and was the blackest turkey I ever saw. His terminal band was the exact color of the huckleberry stems, and his upper tail coverts were the color of the dead straw under the bushes. I had killed what the oldtimers refer to as a mosseyheaded gobbler.

I wish I knew more about the mosseyheaded gobblers (turkeys). What exactly are they? Maybe they could thrive in all these thickets the timber companies are creating.

Colonel Bill Hornsey and Mr. Murray Wilson have both passed away since the little gobbler in Uncle Percy's thicket gave us so much entertainment. A timber company owns the place now and "silviculture" has destroyed all the huckleberry bushes, the creek bottom is a jungle of briars and the big stands of hardwood are gone. Times have changed drastically.

* * * * *

Miscellaneous Facts/Opinions

The range of a wild turkey flock is dictated primarily by food supply. A flock with an abundant food supply will travel less distance than a flock with a marginal supply of food sources.

Turkeys are efficient at gleaning foods from apparently barren landscapes. Turkeys eat a large variety of foods. It is hard to discover something which they will not eat. The low grade quality foods will sustain a flock even though better food is preferred.

The rate of metabolism of young turkeys is extremely high and the youngsters need to feed regularly and often. Young turkeys need a lot of protein in their diets. Providing them with high carbohydrate diets artificially is inviting disaster.

Juvenile hens nest during their first spring.

Flock composition during the feeding period (fall and winter) is dictated by the social status of individuals within a flock. The peck order is very strong and this accounts for young gobblers hanging together and old gobblers remaining in small groups. Hens with young of the year will be together and some late hatched gobblers of the year will remain with the hen flocks.

The periods of the year are as follows: Mating, Nesting, Brooding, Molting, Feeding, and Congregation. These turkey events are the seasonal periods which are brought about by the nature of the wild turkey's annual cycle. The congregation period is in late winter when food is scarce and large flocks made of all ages and both sexes ready themselves for the mating period. The periods overlap with each preceding and succeeding period.

* * * * *

"Dad and BJ"

"Coyotes, Game Enemy #1"

8 A Very Weird Hunt

One might consider all gobbler hunts to be unique in one way or another. In dealing with this reptillian type of feathered creature, the hunter will often best prepare himself by expecting the exception to be the rule, or ruling out the expected in favor of the unexpected—if that makes any sense.

No kidding, the reason turkey hunting becomes such a passion with certain types of us lies within the very nature of the quarry. He is a strange bird, and strange birds would necessarily produce some strange hunts.

I have been a party to some weird hunts, but the strangest of them all involved a pretty morning hunt some years ago when things in the woods seemed unusual. Here is my account of that weird hunt.

A big fine gobbler followed a group of hens down a ridge road at sunset returning to the deep woods from a pasture where they had been feeding that late afternoon. Their pace was hurried as they hastened towards the area where the group habitually roosted.

The big gobbler parted from the hens and dropped off to the west. He flew up to roost on a little creek and changed limbs exactly once. The hens walked out in a pine thicket to the east, and, one by one, flew also to roost, each of them changing limbs several times. The gobbler was separated from his contingent of females by about two hundred yards.

PERFECT!

The next morning, at least a solid hour before daylight, I stood like a statue in the inky blackness halfway between the gobbler and the hens. Admittedly, I was feeling quite smug about my position, even though my guts dictated that I should have been at home asleep.

As the east became a little gray, and my eyes had become adjusted, I saw very clearly a large deer standing within ten feet of me. Soon it was apparent that the animal was totally unaware of me. The deer finally moved away at a very casual pace.

Moments later, the large deer was replaced in the gloom by two small deer; I saw them look at each other and sniff the air and look at each other again. The pair of young ones took up the trail of the big deer at the same unhurried rate and in a couple of seconds, were swallowed up by the cover and darkness. None of the three animals made a sound which was audible to my ears.

I took a deep breath and thought about sitting down on the pine needle carpet under my feet, but the thought of rattlers and moccasins made the idea a very fleeting one. I have learned to be aware of where one sits in this country. I continued to stand still. I practiced focusing on objects for ten seconds or so at a time while looking out of the corners of my eyes. Time crept by and the gray in the east became brighter.

I really don't know how long after the two small deer had passed when another animal showed up on the assembly spot of the three previous animals. Another animal followed this one, followed by another and another and yet another until there were five new animals standing less than ten feet from me. All of them sort of huddled on the spot before also sniffing the air like the other ones did.

The group of animals had vanished ghostlike in the pre-dawn light before I realized that they were not deer. They had to have been either dogs or coyotes—and big ones too. I had the thought that they were entirely too quiet to be dogs. They made no sound at all.

In fact there was no noise at all in the woods, except for the soft humming of an oil well off in the distance. No owls hooted. No insects buzzed. No toads sang. Nothing happened as daylight came. No gobbling either. No flying down. No yelping. I still stood like a tree—no calling. Not even a crow made a noise.

I finally sat down, thoroughly bemused by the situation. The weather was good; it was clear and very little humidity hung in the morning cool. What a mystery was developing. And I sat still for two hours without hearing any living creatures or seeing so much as a squirrel after daylight entered with its wonderful illumination. I did hear a wood thrush flute out a single spring time phrase and then he was quiet too.

Some two hours after sunrise, I was still quite alert in spite of no activity. It was not as though the woods were asleep, but I had the distinct feeling that great evil was afoot some how or other. The woodland creatures seemed to relay that the whole community was poised and ready for some major event or something. I put these silly thoughts out of my head and rose to my feet and with measured stalking steps walked back the way I had come.

Way off to the west, the direction all the pre-dawn animals had traveled, I heard the signal bark of a dog coyote. For some reason, all the hair on the back of my neck stood erect, and I immediately walked in the direction of the bark. Two other barks from different male coyotes were heard as I approached a high bank overlooking an old logging road which ran through a thicket. I, for once, made no noise as I approached, my shotgun at port arms.

I stopped about one hundred feet from the road to light a cigarette.

The breeze was blowing in my face. By easing forward a few feet at a time, I gained the top of the bank quietly and stood there for a few minutes concealed from the west by the brow of the bank itself. The shapes and forms within the thicket below began to become images.

A large brown coyote was lying down in the middle of the log road. Some fifty feet beyond him and about seventy yards from me stood two very dark coyotes. All three animals were facing in my direction. I didn't move and the coyotes didn't either. Shortly I became aware of some small noises almost directly beneath me at the foot of the bank.

Looking down, I spotted two more coyotes; one of them was looking directly into my eyes. The other one was feeding on a freshly killed deer. I would have bet even money that the deer was one of the small deer I had seen before daylight.

Just like shooting a gobbler, I raised my shotgun, put the bead on the tip of the nose of the coyote looking at me, and squeezed the trigger. The animal dropped like he had a rug pulled out from under him. My second shot caught the rear end of the other coyote which had been feeding on the deer. He did not fall, but ran sideways in a big semicircle out through the thicket. The other three 'yotes had disappeared. I looked the dead coyote over, being amazed at how the parasites left his body within three minutes of the cessation of his heart beat.

I felt good about killing one of them, but wished that I could have caught them all on the carcass. I might have waited a minute if that one coyote hadn't been looking right at me. The thought of such an uneventful morning becoming useful made my day. But my day was not yet over.

Now please bear in mind that all of this deer killing and shooting of coyotes had taken place within four hundred yards of where I knew a big gobbler had been roosting. I assumed that the gobbler had done a silent fly-down and was a long ways from there by now. The thought of hooking up in a duel with that gobbler was the farthest thing from my mind as I returned to my original stand of the pre-dawn before starting back to the truck.

The hum of the oil well was still smooth to the north. Every once in a while I could hear a metallic clank from some piece of machinery on the working rig. The well was, perhaps, two miles from the spot I occupied.

Suddenly, a very high pitched pinging sound came from the oil well. I learned after that the sound had been that of a large section of pipe falling and hitting the decking below. I also learned later that the pipe had struck a workman and crushed him to death. There was no way for me to know what happened at the time. All I knew was that the gobbler was still on the roost and let forth with a tremendous gobble when the pipe fell. It was after nine o'clock in the morning, and the turkey had apparently been stimulated by the high pitch tone of the metal pipe hitting the steel decking.

Immediately, the hens all began to yelp and cackle. This, after hours of sitting in their roost trees without making a sound. I was amazed. The gobbler continued to gobble from the roost and one by one, I heard the hens begin to fly down.

I was already back in my original position and did not sit, but just stood there in awe of what was going on. The gobbler walked right up to the first call I made after flying about half the distance to me. I killed him just as dead as a door knob with the last shell in my gun. He was a beautiful gobbler.

Mine were the only shots fired within five miles of the place I hunted. In fact, of a dozen or so hunters, I was the only person who reported even hearing a turkey gobble. And strangely, half of the other hunters had observed or heard coyotes that morning.

* * * * *

Miscellaneous Facts/Opinions

Twelve to fifteen eggs in the first clutch of the year for an adult hen is most common. The second laying will invariably contain fewer eggs. Wild turkey hens have been observed on nests as late as October.

Nest abandonment occurs most often while the hen is still laying and not actually in the process of incubation. Some hens will allow themselves to be chopped up by mowers and pasture clippers if they have already begun to incubate their eggs at the time of such mishaps.

* * * * *

PART TWO

Calling, Hunting, and Peculiarities of the Wild Turkey

"Morgan Caller"

9 The Art of Calling Springtime Gobblers

Many volumes of literature have been written on the subject of wild turkeys. Most modern day books are very well written and are thoroughly documented. By reading the books available now, you can find out what the birds look like, what they eat, how long it takes for their eggs to hatch, how densely populated they are in one region or another; you can find out just about anything you want to know about the wild turkey.

However, very few accounts truly tell you how you might call one of these grand trophies to your shotgun. And no wonder, the actual methods of calling gobblers is a very difficult subject to write about. The turkey gobbler can present you with such a myriad of situations and with so many decisions to make until there may be an overload created on the brain.

The truth of the matter is that there is no certain way a hunter can be assured of calling up a gobbler anytime. Even when you know where the gobbler is located and know what his pattern is, the bird has a way of escaping cleanly. More specifically, he may shun your calling attempts completely.

Being reasonable people, you and I need to be somewhat systematic in our approach to calling gobblers. Never mind that our scientific plans will often run aground. At least we will have given it our best shot. When that occasional monarch of the deep woods makes us look really bad, we can rest assured that our Creator has presented us with one of his creations to help us master our own egos.

I suppose we should begin with an examination of the different types of turkey calling instruments. Just about all turkey hunters have their own preferred type of caller which they like to use when it gets right down to the nitty gritty of killing a trophy gobbler. I am a little partial to the one I patented years ago. I can do more things with it than any other brand or type of caller.

Make no mistake that I won't be the first in line to get a caller of any type which I can use to make any particular turkey hunting sound better than anything which I may be using currently. I have noticed that most callers have a specialty sound, a sound which that caller can imitate better than any of the other types. Nowadays, I use eight different noise making devices in my attempts to call gobblers. I would feel seriously handicapped without any of them. Over the years, I have used no fewer than fifty different brands and types.

Most fishermen have a box full of fishing lures because they know fish don't hit the same bait every day. It's the same kind of deal with turkey hunters and turkey callers. Gobblers just don't react the same way every day.

On some days a gobbler will absolutely run right over a box caller sound and on other days, they will do the same for a diaphragm caller. Sometimes any friction caller will scare turkeys completely out of the country. There are times when soft calling won't arouse the birds and yet the loud calls will set them to gobbling like crazy. Then there are days when gobblers will only tolerate the softest of sounds. One particular caller will work nicely on gobblers for a few trials, then the birds of an area won't be fooled by that device for the rest of the season. Gobblers like to gobble at owl hooting. In some areas which may have been 'over owled', the first imitation of a barred owl will make all gobblers within hearing shut up completely. These same owl shy birds may gobble at a hawk call though.

The crux of the whole matter is that the serious turkey hunter is far ahead of the game if he can master more than one type of caller. The more versatile the calling, the better. A real turkey hunter needs to be able to imitate a variety of sounds which the wild turkey uses in the every day language of the flock.

Box callers are easy callers to use. That is they are easy to make sounds with. The box caller makes a decent yelp and one or two other sounds. In all honesty, the box caller is used primarily by hunters who do not have the confidence or fortitude to master other kinds of callers. There are a few successful hunters who actually prefer the box, but they are few and far between. Turkeys wise up to box callers quicker than most other kinds of callers and these callers are useless in wet weather.

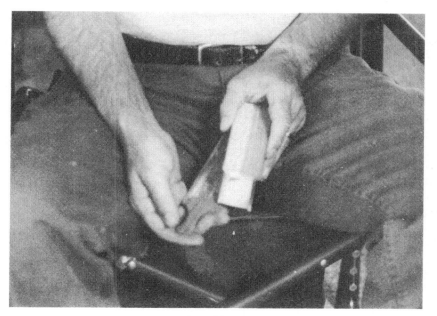

"Box Caller"

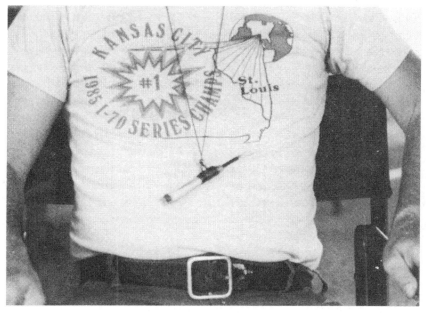

"Wingbone Caller"

Yet, the box will often call gobblers which won't begin to show interest in other callers.

The wingbone caller is tried and true. The claims made by some veteran hunters that the wingbone caller has caused the death of more old gobblers than any other caller just might be true. This instrument is difficult to master and really makes only one call real well. The wingbone makes a perfect lonesome hen yelp and a pretty fair tree yelp. These callers can be heard a great distance through the woods.

The Morgan Caller is a versatile caller which is difficult to operate. It makes an excellent cackle and a very good gobble imitation. Of course it is my favorite caller. Other tube type callers are either made out of plastic or are engineered with the wrong parameters for producing sounds like this one. I use other calls to cluck, purr, and tree yelp with because they make better purrs, clucks, and tree yelps than my caller. No caller can imitate the gobble as well as this one. It takes much practice to master this instrument.

The slate callers are good callers for producing clucks, purrs, and the quaver of the quiet hen. Many varieties of slate and peg callers are available. You need to call with them outside before you buy one to see what kind of resonating force they have in their sound production. Some slate callers sound much better inside than outside. Use a pocket knife to roughen the surface of the slate or glass for friction points. Late in the season, the quiet slate out-performs all other instruments for me.

Mouth yelpers may be the most popular callers in America today. They can be used without moving your eyes or hands. Some people can make very realistic calls with mouth yelpers. The double staggered reed mouth yelper makes an excellent assembly yelp of the old hen. Any caller having rubber parts should be kept in the refrigerator when it is not in use. This will prolong the life of the rubber parts. Tilting the head backwards a little while calling will open your air ways and produce sound sources from deeper inside your throat and make for better turkey sounds. Store bought diaphragms are good in about one out of ten purchases. They are all different no matter how much care the manufacturer takes in their production.

The fully feathered turkey wing is a device used for imitating the flying down 'fluff fluff' sound of turkeys. Follow your tree yelping with 'fluff fluffing' and you may get dramatic results. A cackle following your wing flapping may land a gobbler on top of you. Treat your wings and dry them properly and the same wing may last for a number of years.

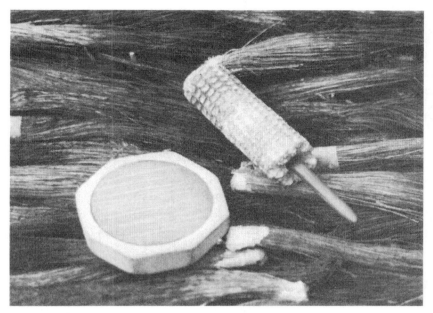

"Slate Caller"

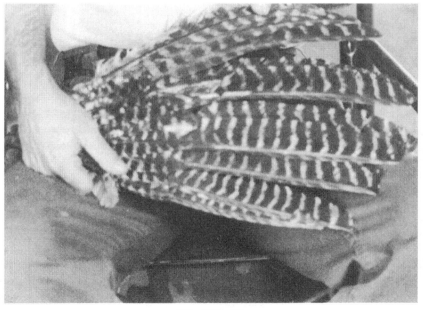

"Fluff Fluff"

Use the left wing with your left hand, and the right wing with your right hand.

I only carry one wing into the woods with me and hold my shotgun in the other while I am 'fluff fluffing'. Do not have anything loose in your clothing when you imitate the flying down of a turkey. Nickels and dimes and pocket knives do not usually clank when a real turkey flies down. The best noise to make is three long and violent strokes and about five shorter strokes with decreasing violence. That's the way a hen turkey sounds much of the time when she lands from the roost.

The vocabulary of the wild turkey needs to be examined so at least we can be together on our terminology. I will list only those calls of the wild turkey with which I am familiar. There may be some rackets of the birds not listed. Some folks describe sounds and make noises with turkey callers which I have never heard. I would strongly suggest that you listen to real turkeys at every opportunity—wild turkeys if at all possible. I have heard recordings which were clearly tame turkeys.

Sometimes, word descriptions of the various calls are inadequate, but I will try to give you an idea of what the sounds are like. I will also include a rough idea of how the sounds fit into calling plans.

Yelping

Yelping is the most common form of communication among turkeys. There are several kinds of yelps and they may be recognized after you hear them a few times.

Tree Yelps are short nasal yelps with a quick little tempo having three to eight notes per series of calls. These soft yelps are emitted by turkeys very early in the morning, often while it is too dark to see the ground. Hens, especially, use this sort of comunication to reassure themselves that there are indeed other members of the flock close by. In a hunting situation, it is a good call to use after you have roosted a big gobbler the evening before. I like to make the tree yelp about three or four times just about the time the towhees begin to sing at dawn, but only when I know exactly where the gobbler is roosting. I used to make the sound every morning, but I found that it is tough to start your calling before good light only to learn all too soon that a big gobbler is roosted right over your head. You will find that gobblers do not answer the tree yelp as readily as some of the other calls, but they most assuredly will come to where you make this call. Be prepared at all times when you imitate the tree yelp. A gobbler may swoop down on top of you.

Conversational Yelps are exchanged among members of a moving, feeding flock. These flat monotoned yelps are usually accompanied by some contentment purring as the flock keeps in close touch with each other as they feed along. If I am well hidden and a group of turkeys moves by, I will use the conversational yelp to try to entice the whole band to swing by closer to me. In the early part of most spring turkey seasons, you may see five or six hens leading a big old gobbler around. The conversational yelp probably does not work that much better than any of the other sounds for getting the whole bunch close to you, but I have a lot of confidence in it and it can be imitated with a number of types of callers.

The Lonesome Hen Yelp is also known as the plain hen yelp. It is a five to ten note call which has an inquisitive or plaintif tone as if to ask, Where are you? This is the call turkeys use if they do not get together immediately after flying down from their roosts and starting toward the feeding grounds. It is the standard call to make at any gobbler at any time when hunting.

The Assembly Yelp and *The Lost Yelp* are very similar in sound. The assembly yelp of old hens proceeds with each note being the same as the notes preceding; whereas the lost yelp seems to increase in urgency and there is a perceptible rise in pitch in each succeeding note. The lost yelp of young turkeys is often accompanied by the Kee Kee Kee whistling types of sounds. The assembly yelp is usually raspy and loud; both calls are demands upon other members of the flock to gather close by the sound producer. Loud assembly calling early in a turkey season is very effective in calling unseasoned gobblers. Gobblers get wise to this type of calling in a hurry, no matter what kind of device you may choose to imitate the sound with, simply because the entire flock knows the voice of the assembly hen of that group.

Quavers are extremely soft yelps which are very slow in rhythm. For reasons unknown to me, most series of quavers contain exactly three notes. The call is used by turkeys which have lost visual contact with their companions in dense cover. It is a quiet 'come here' sort of sound. It is a deadly call to use on a gobbler which may have hung up just out of sight.

Clucks/Putts

These important communications sounds are poorly understood. While each variety of cluck and putt does have a slightly different sound, *it is the sequence and circumstances of their use which tells other turkeys what is going on*. Clucks and putts may best be described as sharp sudden call notes akin to the sound of an acorn falling into water.

Assembly Clucks are single notes less than one half of a second long. The pitch is slightly higher at the end of each note. The assembly cluck of a mature gobbler sounds like a stick striking a hollow log. Both hens and gobblers use the assembly cluck to signal a 'come here' disposition to unseen partners of the species. When using this cluck or any other, it is a safe bet to put other turkey sounds with it. I.e., a cluck followed by a quaver, or a cluck followed by a purr.

Identification Clucks are very similar to alarm putts and usually contain only a couple of notes. Turkeys use this sound to demand upon the intruder to identify itself. *Alarm Putts* are even sharper than ID clucks and there may be several notes of alarm. The alarm putt can change into ID clucks and back to alarm putts again at the whim of the turkey making the sound. The ID clucks accompanied by warning purrs are not nearly as serious as a couple of putts followed by silence. A couple of these ID clucks or putts will make smart gobblers several hundred yards away stand up and listen and look for as long as an hour.

Pitts are like mini putts, but have no resonance and are light textured. These sounds are usually heard coming from nervous turkeys on the roost. Pitts can change into cutts when these nervous turkeys are about to fly down.

Cackles/Cutts

Cackles are staccato series of sharp clucking sounds which go up and then down again in pitch. Usually only one or two yelps follow the rapid series in a flying up to roost situation. Sometimes fifteen or twenty full fledged yelps will follow the cackle series in a flying down from the roost situation. The fast *cut-cut sounds* associated with yelping indicate impatience on the part of the turkeys. There are times when agitated, nervous, or worried turkeys will make a series of cutts which sound like putts, clucks, and pitts, all rolled into one series. Any of these excited sounds may bring a response from a big tom at any time of the day. They may also make a big tom skedaddle. These sounds, the cackle and the cutts, also are picked up on quickly by gobblers. For that matter, I guess any sound can be picked up on by a wise gobbler.

Purrs

There are several kinds of purring noises emitted by turkeys in several situations. Each purr is unique and has a different meaning.

Contentment Purrs are very high pitched sounds lasting about one second each. The beginning and the end of this purr has the same pitch. A true contentment purr cannot be heard by a human more than one hundred feet. Of course turkeys make purrs a little louder at times, but this is normally a very quiet communication among turkeys which are together. A cluck followed by a purr is a deadly call to use on springtime gobblers. I like to vary the resonance factor of my clucks and purrs so that the calling seems to be moving around and sounds like more than one turkey.

Warning Purrs or *Investigative Purrs* are louder and longer than contentment purrs and the pitch at the end of each note is higher than that of the beginning. Turkeys which have spotted something out of the ordinary will emit this warning purr and they will couple that with ID clucks, not so urgent putts, and even yelps. As their source of agitation increases, so will the urgency and loudness of this type of purring. *Aggravated Purrs* are even louder, longer, and much harsher than the warning purr. This call denotes anger. It too is accompanied by clucks, cutts, and all sorts of noises. Gobblers in particular, sound off in this fashion when a fight is in the making. An imitation of the aggravated purr followed by the imitation of a young gobbler's gobble will sometimes make an old boss gobbler come right to you.

Kee Kee Notes

Kee-Kee-Kee is an apt description of the call notes of the very young turkeys of the year. Even after turkeys mature, especially hens, they may retain these whistling sounds as part of their calling. Kee Kee notes are often heard prior to all sorts of yelps. Kee Kee sounds ahead of your imitations may add a little flavor to your calling if you are proficient at making them.

Singing Sounds

Turkeys make a wide variety of little noises when they are loafing, dusting, and feeding. They are invariably soft little rackets with no set pattern. One of these little sounds can be described as the phrase 'yew—yew——yew—yew——yew—yew' in a high nasal voice. If you can imitate one of these sounds exactly like a wild turkey, it will be helpful in assuring an old monarch that you are the real McCoy.

Gobbling

Gobbling is the sound which we go to the woods to hear. It is well known that turkeys gobble just because they feel like it. They also use the gobble to alert hens to their whereabouts. The gobble is also a vocal challenge to other gobblers within hearing or sight. Each age group of gobblers can be identified by their gobble calls.

Jakes or one year old gobblers can best be described as having a guttural gobble with all the notes running together in a jumbled fashion. Jakes are sporadic gobblers; they do not have a set pattern like the old gobblers; they gobble when the mood strikes them. When jakes become aroused, they can be among the noisiest creatures on earth. They are very stupid during their first spring and it is a sin to shoot one of them.

Two Year Old Gobblers have a gobble which has a very distinct first note, a sort of CUTT! at the beginning of the call. These birds are not usually dominant in an area, so are constantly jockeying for a better position in the peck order. They gobble aggressively and are easily led to a caller. When two or more gobblers of this age group are together, they will sometimes gobble simultaneously. I don't know how they accomplish this. Assembly calls are deadly on two year old birds. I have seen two year old gobblers with eleven inch beards and with spurs more than an inch long.

Three Year Old Gobblers or mature gobblers have gobbles which have distinctly separate notes throughout the call. You can hear each note individually. Some four year old gobblers sound like this and some two year old toms also have this kind of gobble. The gobbling of mature gobblers is usually loud. The mature birds are on top of the peck order in their part of the world. They may accept younger birds in their presence during the spring if the younger toms show no threats or signs of mating behavior. Mature gobblers can often be enraged by imitating the sounds of another gobbler.

Old Monarchs more than four years of age have been lucky or real good at what they do. These turkeys are real sharp, their gobbles being shrill sounds with rattle effects on the end. Six year old birds and older sound like a shaking can full of ball bearings when they gobble. The quiet approach is best on these turkeys. Unless you have a pair of old buddies who have been together from day one, the old monarch does not normally accept stragglers or intermediate aged gobblers at their sides in the spring or winter. You will find that these old birds will have a set pattern to their daily activities most of the time. They can be extremely difficult to call and getting one of these longbeards is quite a feat.

Squawking/Screeching

The screeching or squawking of a wild turkey is a wild sound. It sounds something like a startled Great Blue Heron. The sound is made by toms who have been waiting for that elusive little hen to show up and have grown tired of waiting. The impatience shown by a screeching gobbler is not to be taken lightly. These gobblers are among the slickest you will ever encounter. My pulse rate quickens when I hear a gobbler squawk, because I know that he must be a dandy turkey. Some veteran hunters consider the screech to be an aborted gobble or just the high frequency portion of a gobble.

Drumming/Strutting

The 'Pfffft!' 'Vvrroooooom' sound emitted by a male turkey is an amazing sound. The 'Pffft!' portion is completely independent of the 'Vvrroooooom' part and the two different sounds are sometimes made *independently* of each other. Sometimes an old gobbler will only make one of the two sounds. It is not necessary for the gobbler to be in the strutting posture for him to make either of these sounds. At times the gobbler will emit the "Vvrroooooom' sound while he is just walking along. Maybe they use this sound to attract hens—I don't know. A hunter with good hearing can hear a turkey drum about one hundred yards away.

Tactics

It is more important to deal with how you approach your quarry than it is to select the correct call. The mode of approach will depend upon one or more of several factors. Let's examine some of the more influential factors.

Gobbler Personalities

All gobblers have a personality; they exhibit certain behavioral traits which label them. Of course gobblers may show more than one personality and may even change personalities within a single season.

A *Suspicious* natured gobbler is among the hardest of all gobblers to call. He is the gobbler which often shuts up all gobbling when you call to him. This type of turkey should be called very softly. You should not set up to call him any closer than two hundred yards from where he gobbles. When the suspicious gobbler is in full view, no calling at all should be attempted.

A *Quiet Gobbler*, one that does little or no gobbling, is also a difficult and aggravating thing to fool with. Only one type of caller and one call of the turkey should be used per encounter with the quiet ones. A quiet gobbler may know of your whereabouts and since he is quiet, stands a good chance of sneaking up on you. If you use all your calls and callers, he will become educated very fast. Then he won't even sneak up to you for a look.

A *Noisy Longbeard* works best if you raise him into a frenzy and then cease all calling completely. Try cutting off his gobbles with your own calling. When he quits gobbling—Look out! He is on his way to you.

An *Aggressive Tom* is one which marches boldly along and is hostile to all other gobblers. This kind of gobbler is easy prey to imitations of other gobbler sounds. Sometimes it is necessary to set up close to aggressive gobblers so you will be sure you are close enough to make him feel threatened by your gobbler imitations.

A *Reclusive Gobbler* is best defined as a bird which spends most of his time in a very small area. Careful approach is the key here. If you can set up on this turkey undetected within a hundred yards or so of that favorite little place of his, you will have good luck. What kind of calling you do won't matter too much. These reclusive gobblers are fun to fool with because you know where they will be. Their whole spring may be spent on a scant one hundred acre lot.

A *Vagabond or Circuit Riding Gobbler* is the exact opposite of the reclusive gobbler. He likes to ramble all over the whole country. He may have a circuit of three miles or more. Often they will answer your calling and all the while be moving on to their next stop. These turkeys are a lot of fun to fool with if you like hiking across the country. Keep circling ahead of the turkey and eventually you will wind up in a spot he wants to be. Sometimes you can follow this sort of turkey and he will suddenly turn right around and come back to you. Loud calls are in order here to illicit responses from the turkey so you can keep track of him. I use a hawk call to make these turkeys gobble. Sometimes there is nothing you can do to steer them off course.

Seasonal Factors

Early in the spring, turkeys of both sexes are much more vocal than they are during the later part of the spring. Gobblers have several periods of high gobbling activity, but hunting pressure, more than anything else, quietens them down. Hens become quieter as their roosting groups become fewer in number with each passing day of spring. The business of egg laying and finally, incubation of clutches, does away with all the cackling and assembly calls of the early season. Groups of hens whose nests have been destroyed may regroup and make some early spring sounds, but this is the exception rather than the rule. Your calling needs to tailor itself to meet the mode of the season. It's not a good idea to call too loudly late in the season unless you find a tom which insists on being a noisy character. The late season foliage may keep you from hearing turkeys for any great distance, but the greenery may also allow you to approach closer than earlier.

Time of the Day Factors

I have never seen any evidence that the time of day makes any difference when it comes to calling turkeys. While it may be true that real hens are noisier during the early morning hours, loud calling is effective during the mid day hours and by the same token, the soft calls are too. Don't be too concerned about what time of day it is; if a gobbler is ready, he is ready.

Calling Efficiency Factors

I have mentioned that a hunter is ahead of his game if he can master more than one caller and learn to imitate more than one call of the wild turkey. This will help. However, let me point out that you should resort to that caller and turkey sound which you are the most proficient with during critical situations. If your plain hen yelping is better with a mouth diaphragm than with a box, then yelp with a mouth yelper. Rely heavily on your best call. Put your best foot forward. If you don't cluck and purr real well, then don't attempt to cluck and purr with a big old gobbler standing out there in front of you. If you can gobble real good, then do a lot of gobbling.

Experience Factors

This is a simple factor. If I call to a gobbler by cackling and he shuts up, I am not going to cackle at him anymore. If I get close to a gobbler and he moves away from me, then I am not going any closer. If I moo like a cow and the gobbler answers me like crazy, then I am going to moo some more. Use your prior experiences to your advantage.

Desire Factors

When a hunter of any substance at all has killed a nice gobbler or two, his desire to kill more game wanes. Take this opportunity to experiment with gobblers you may be working. Since it really doesn't matter whether you kill the bird or not, you may be astonished at what you can discover about these birds.

Position Factors

If I am not in the place where I want to be, or if I am not hidden properly, I don't like to call at all. If I do weaken and call from what I consider to be a poor position, out of habit, I will move away from there whether I get an answer from the gobbler I am working or not. It is a rough deal when you get ambushed by a gobbler; don't think they won't sneak up on you.

Confusion Factors

A confused hunter sometimes will just get plain lucky. When I am confused about what to do, I just pull out any old caller and make whatever sound comes to mind. I have killed a good many gobblers like that.

Here is a chart which I have devised to help you make some of those more rational decisions.

Turkey Sound	Situation
Tree yelp	Roosted gobblers
Lonesome hen yelp	Any gobbler, anytime
Assembly yelp/Lost yelp	Two year old gobblers Noisy gobblers Early season gobblers Circuit riders/Vagabond gobblers
Cutts/Cackle	Early season gobblers Locator attempts Keep track of vagabond gobblers Gobblers with hens
Cluck and purr	Suspicious gobblers Quiet gobblers Hung up gobblers Late season gobblers
Quaver	Suspicious gobblers Thick cover gobblers Hung up gobblers Late season gobblers
Conversation yelp	Gobblers following hens Gobblers which fly down close by Gobblers within sight
Gobbling	Aggressive gobblers Dominant gobblers

Please accept this chart for what it is. It is an attempt to summarize the methods which I use in actually calling turkeys. This is not to say that any of the calls of the wild turkey will or won't work in any situation. I believe you could pull a rusty nail out of a board sometimes and the danged things would run over you. If they are ready to come to a caller, you can't run them away. The following preparations which will be described are just as important in getting a springtime gobbler as calling. I have known a good many hunters who could call just fine, but had a great deal of difficulty getting the drop on any kind of gobbler. The business of calling gobblers is just one aspect of hunting. It is an important part of sport hunting. Hunting the wild gobbler without a turkey caller would take away much of the fun we have in chasing them around.

Checklist for Calling Springtime Gobblers

1. Master as many different types of callers as possible
2. Learn to imitate as many different turkey sounds as possible
3. Learn to identify the different age groups of gobblers
4. Learn the meaning of different turkey sounds
5. Train your ear to hear the drumming sounds
6. Call suspicious gobblers softly
7. Stay a comfortable distance from suspicious gobblers when preparing to call
8. Do no calling when a suspicious gobbler is in full view
9. Use only one caller per encounter with a quiet gobbler
10. Call loudly and aggressively to a noisy gobbler
11. Cut off a noisy gobbler with your own calling
12. Cease calling when you have a noisy gobbler hot and bothered
13. Use gobbler imitations on an aggressive gobbler
14. Set up as close as possible to an aggressive gobbler
15. Get in the middle of a reclusive gobbler's baliwick; get where he lives
16. Try following a vagabond gobbler
17. Try circling ahead of a vagabond gobbler
18. Call loudly early in the season
19. Call softly late in the season
20. Use your best caller in critical situations
21. Do not repeat mistakes with your experiences
22. Experiment with gobblers which you have no desire to kill
23. Do not call from a bad position or improper hiding place
24. Do not call the preferred male more than once or twice while he is still on the roost*
25. When confused do not be shy about calling, anything might work

---

* See Chapter Twelve on "The Preferred Male Gobbler"

"Antique Callers, courtesy of Jimmy Koepp"

"You'll be surprised at what you can observe."

10 Stealth

Johnny Dale, IV of Natchez and I went hunting on one of my favorite places a few years ago. A very nice gobbler and several lesser gobblers began to gobble at first light across a pasture from where Johnny and I were listening. We delayed our departure to those woods where all the gobbler talk was coming from. We were waiting for another gobbler to sound off in the close vicinity to where we already were stationed. The close gobbler never opened his mouth, even though I knew he was somewhere in the neighborhood.

We became more interested in all the gobbling going on in the big woods across the pasture. Finally, we decided to go ahead and take our chances with the gobblers already making noise. We circled around under a hill so the biggest gobbler, which was roosting right on the opposite edge of the pasture, would not be able to see us cross the opening. We were in too big of a hurry. As we approached the field crossing, we spotted a group of deer standing on top of the hill directly between us and the oldest gobbler. The deer had to be in plain sight of the gobbler, and the deer were in plain sight of us. The gobbler could not see us where we were.

After watching the deer in the pasture a few minutes, I decided to cross the field anyway. Of course the deer bolted into the woods between us and the turkey. We neither saw nor heard that particular old gobbler the rest of the morning. Even though we played with and called up several other gobblers, the one we went after just gave us the slip—all because I was not content to wait a while longer and let the deer go on their way of their own accord.

There are a great number of things which can go wrong to cause you to *not* be toting a big gobbler out of the woods on any given morning. It is truly incredible how many things can foul up a hunt. Some ill fated hunts are caused by factors beyond our control; a tree could even fall and scare your turkey. But many situations arise to plug up the works which are of our own doing. In order to be more consistently successful at turkey hunting, you must develop the following skills and attitudes:

1. You must not be in a hurry.
2. You must be lucky.
3. You must learn to blend into the woods scene.
4. You must be quiet when moving and waiting.
5. You must be alert and recognize game sights and sounds.
6. You must recognize good places to hide and wait for a gobbler.
7. You must be able to shoot a gobbler when the time is right.
8. You must know how to shoot a gobbler correctly.
9. You must learn to turn down bad shot offerings.
10. You must pass up some gobblers which present themselves to be shot, and you must share your opportunities with your friends.

Patience

Of all the attitudes and/or skills, the hardest one to accomplish is the posture of not being in any kind of rush. Very few gobblers are bagged by hunters who are in a hurry. If you have pressing business on the morning of your hunt, make up your mind not to go at all or decide that you must leave the woods on time as planned.

If you should decide to go ahead with your hunt, carry out your hunt as if you had the whole day to hunt. Do all the things necessary to make a good hunt at the same pace every time you go into the woods after turkeys. The gobbler is not likely to be going anywhere unless he gets spooked or killed. A hunter in a hurry is most likely to spook him and least likely to kill him.

If your game plan calls for waiting at a spot, then go wait at that spot as long as you have time to wait. If it is necessary to take an hour to get to that spot without being detected, then take the full hour to make your way there. If you don't have an hour, then forget it until you do have the time to do it right.

The amount of time taken in getting in position to kill a gobbler is equal to the amount of time it should take for you to get away from an unsuccessful attempt to call a gobbler. That's right, it is just as important to leave a place at a slow pace as it is to approach a spot with stealth. Be slow and deliberate in your movements both to and from a hunting area.

Lady luck

You need Lady Luck on your side to be good at any game. Any mature gobbler which gets killed has encountered a hunter with some kind of old fashioned luck on his side.

I always tell my basketball players that the harder they play, the luckier they will be. I believe that. I know several turkey hunters who can't call worth a flip, and they are not that good as still hunters either. Some of them are even noisy in the woods, yet they kill gobblers pretty regularly because they stay after the birds; they eventually get lucky.

Your luck will also increase many times if you are generous with your hunting buddies and share your secrets and whereabouts of gobblers with them. I have been extremely lucky by assuming this attitude. Naturally, you don't need too dad gum many hunting buddies to share all your secrets with. But many hunters are too selfish to have any good luck at all.

Of course, mastering the skills involved in hunting will go a long way in making you a luckier hunter. How many times have you heard folks comment on how lucky one hunter or another is? A lot of that luck is surely plain luck, but a lot of lucky success is created by the hunter doing something right. Hunting is a numbers game and the more of those numbers you eliminate by developing the skills which go with turkey hunting, the better are your odds of scoring.

Blending In

Blending into the scenery is an art in itself. Over the years we have picked up on some things which enable an alien creature to the woods, like man the hunter, to mesh with the woods picture much more effectively. Not being in a hurry begins the process of being part of the woods and not alien to it.

Horizontal lines presented by any part of your anatomy and/or clothing are much more likely to be spotted by wild game than are lines which appear rounded or vertical. Hats with flat horizontal bills or tops are very easy for turkeys to spot. Your hunting coat should be free of outstanding lines which are horizontal. Even the short lines of some coat pockets do not fit in. The edges of some coats accent those tell tale horizontal lines.

Of all the things which give the hunter away, the face and hands are most commonly what turkeys recognize first. The hands should always be covered with a soft dark material. If gloves are used, they should be a dark shade and yet still allow you to use your hands. Any hand movement which proceeds from left to right or from right to left (horizontal) is spotted much quicker than hand movements which proceed up and down (vertical). Any movement of the hands needs to be slower than slow.

The face should always be carried in a fashion so that the hunter appears to be looking downward. The upward lifting of your face accents the presence of your eyes and facial features and turkeys are quick to pick up these figures. The wild turkey can literally feel you looking at him when your face is lifted upward. He does not detect one nearly so quickly when your face is tilted downward.

Camouflage of the face can be accomplished very nicely by having each half of your face painted or covered with different tones. If your whole face is mottled in the same pattern, the turkey can still recognize you as a human. If one half is one pattern or color, it is difficult for animals to identify you as a human. Face masks either need to be painted in this manner or they need to be loose. A tight fitting mask of all the same pattern is not effective.

Darker tones are much better than light camouflage tones since the object is to be like a shadow. When a light colored object moves through the woods, it is much more conspicuous than a darker one making the same amount of motion.

Older clothing which has been washed many times is desirable for the quietness of that fabric, but care must be taken so that the clothing has not been thread bared to the extent that it reflects too much light. Real old camo clothing literally glows in the gray light of dawn.

Care must be taken so that you do not become silhouetted against the background of an open field or tree line or even the horizon. When you move around in the turkey woods, take the time to select the proper lanes of travel to move through a piece of terrain. Walking out across an open field is the worst place to travel. In addition to being detected, you will also likely be identified as a human. Hanging strictly on top of an open ridge is also a bad place to be when moving or waiting. Travel in the shadows and you will be much less conspicuous, especially if you have something behind you to break up your silhouette.

Traveling with the light at your back is good if you are not in a position to be skylined. Anyone can see much better looking from an area of relative darkness into an area of relative lightness. A person in a darkened building with the street lights on outside, can easily see someone under the street light, but they cannot see inside the darkened building at all. A turkey looking from the top of a well lighted ridge cannot see objects very well in a darkened hollow by the same principle. Gobblers which are out in openings do not see as effectively if the stalker stays well back in the woods and hangs to the shadowy places. Don't think these advantages will make a hunter completely invisible though and any movement may be detected by wild turkeys at any time.

Author (left) has cap on but has removed face camo—face shines. Van Morgan (center) has face camo, but has removed cap—forehead shines. Keith Thompson (right) is fully camouflaged—no shine at all.

Quiet!

While it is true that turkeys will tolerate noise much better than they will seeing unidentified movement, they can still easily be made suspicious by making undue racket. The worst kind of noise for scaring turkeys is the sound of the human voice. No talking in even a low normal voice will be tolerated by these birds. Whispering is OK if it is a true whisper. Some people must learn to whisper in a sawmill. The human voice factor is one reason why one person can hunt more than twice as effectively as two hunters together. While hunting with a companion, just don't talk. If gobblers frustrate you, please try to avoid talking to yourself until you get out of the woods.

The snapping of sticks alerts every living thing in the woods. Animals which are part of the scene do not break too many sticks accidentally; man does. We all break sticks and twigs when we walk through the woods, but wearing soft soled boots or shoes during the hunt will allow snaps not to be so sharp and crisp when the blunders do occur. A sharply snapping twig is much more alarming than the soft crunching type of stick breaking.

Try placing either the toe or the heel down first when you walk. This mode of travel will take some getting used to, but the margin of error with regards to stepping on dry sticks will be much more tolerable. I take very short steps in the woods when I am stalking along. This slows me down and I can keep my balance much easier like this. But no matter how much we practice at walking in the woods, it is necessary to glance down to see where you are going to put your next step. Step where you look, pause, look around, and look where you will step next. That's the advantage of taking short steps, the movement is less obvious and the rate of travel is much slower. The slower pace allows you to see everything, including those dry sticks which may give you away.

Avoid walking under trees where the conditions would make it impossible to move quietly. The magnolia and sycamore trees have leaves which crackle with the slightest provocation and make all kinds of noise. Stay out from under these types of trees. Detour around them and movement through the woods will be much quieter.

Clothing should be very soft. Animals are alerted by the sound of hard fabric scraping on vegetation. Wool or cotton are ideal materials for hunting clothes. The hard polyester fabrics are difficult to soften enough in order for them to suit my idea of soft clothing.

The swishing sounds of limbs swinging back to positions they occupied before your intrusion also scares turkeys. There are no creatures which make limbs do what some hunters make them do. It is better to get down on your hands and knees and go under a branch than it is to move it suddenly and make a lot of commotion.

As you know, the metallic uniqueness of a safety on a shotgun or rifle scares the living daylights out of all living things. I don't know how, but all the creatures recognize that sound as bad, bad news. Loose change in your pocket will often put turkeys on the alert and the clacking of certain kinds of turkey callers has scared many a gobbler away. Any extraneous noise is picked up by wild turkeys and away they will go.

I have also been in the woods with hunters who insist on clearing their throats. Please don't do that! And if you have to cough, bury your head in your cap or something.

On noise that must be made, it is better to walk at a normal gait through dry woods than it is to make a lot of noise every once in a while. It is important to let the woods get quiet for a period of time after you have necessarily made some noise. If conditions are noisy, then do the best you can. One tip here is that the sound of something walking quietly in water is not nearly as alarming to turkeys as a single crunching sound of gravel under your feet.

Recognize Game Sounds and Sights

The gray squirrel has a special bark for predators, he has another for turkeys and deer, and yet another barking sound he saves for humans. The crow has sort of a 'Crrrraaaaaah' sound he makes when he is bothering a turkey. Deer look at turkeys and then look away quickly. The deer will stare for long moments at almost everything else in the forest.

The turkey sounds somewhat like a man walking through the woods (sometimes). The obvious is not always one hundred percent though, so make sure.

For the sake of hunter safety, you must positively identify game by sight before you even consider making a shot. However, you must be alert to detect the presence of all game when you are hunting turkeys. Being able to recognize the sounds of all the species will save you a lot of time and will also keep you from spooking other animals which will in turn spook the turkey you are after. The wild gobbler is tuned finely with his environment.

When you do recognize the presence of other game, whether by sight or sound, it is very important to let that game continue on its way without alarming it. The snorting of deer has ruined many hunters' chances of getting a gobbler, mine included. I once startled an armadillo which went tearing out through the woods and put a whole flock of turkeys into the air.

Recognize Good Places to Wait

If you are not experienced with a certain piece of turkey real estate, you may be at a loss on deciding exactly where you would like to make your stand to wait for the gobbler. Calling up a gobbler is so very much easier if you can happen up on that spot which is somewhat magical. Some places turkeys won't go and some places they will approach with very little tempting from the caller. Good places to call from

"In the photograph, the left side of road is shadowy—hide there. Stay away from edge and avoid being detected."

are not always apparent and I have found some of them by accident. Other places which I thought would be good did not turn out so good.

Generally, as with moving through the turkey woods, your waiting or hiding place should be looking out of a darkened or shadowy place into a lighted area. I am very fond of hiding just over a rise from the direction of a gobbling or approaching turkey. It is true that the caller has an advantage if he can situate himself on the same ridge with a gobbling turkey. The worst place to be is across some gorge or other physical barrier between you and the turkey.

No matter what the place looks like, if a turkey has been doing a lot of gobbling or strutting there, that's the place to wait. If a turkey gobbles at a spot and then moves off gobbling, be stealthy and get right where the gobbler left from. The turkey will often feel more confident about coming back to a spot where he has already spent some time in an unspooked disposition.

Elaborate blinds are not good in my opinion. Two year old gobblers and the like won't pay much attention to them, but an old wise gobbler will spook from them. This is especially true if he has had the occasion to witness fire belching from such an object.

When waiting for a turkey, sit upright against a tree which is wider than you, if possible. Place your shooting side shoulder against the tree, not your back. Face to your shooting side from where you expect the gobbler to approach. You will have at least 160° for a field of fire without having to move anything except your gun. That 160° will cover anywhere the turkey can appear except directly behind you and the 20° hard by your shooting side.

It is much more comfortable to slouch against the tree and to alternate having one or both of your knees drawn up in front of your body. Rest your gun parallel to your out stretched leg. When action is eminent, but not yet immediate, rest your gun on the knee of your non-shooting side. A few little bushes stuck up out in front of you are good to have. These are only to break up your image and should not be so conspicuous as to draw attention to them. It is still important, in fact even more so, to have your face averted and not lifted upward. Be sure that your cap covers as much of your forehead as will allow you to see out.

The most important aspect of hiding and waiting on a turkey does not involve being hidden properly, even though proper hiding is necessary. The most important aspect of waiting is to keep a constant lookout for the gobbler. Hunters who do not take waiting seriously are not likely to get many gobblers, you must be on the alert for the gobbler at all times. If the turkey gets the drop on you and sees you first, the game is over. If you see him first, you can usually get a good shot no matter how poorly you are hidden.

The fact that you are convinced that you are in the right place will make your wait more relaxing. If the turkey doesn't show, then he doesn't show; you can't do anything about it by fidgeting around.

Shooting the Gobbler

It is sickening to miss a big gobbler and it leads to despair when you hit one and don't get it. We need to make sure of our shots. If a good shot does not present itself, then just don't shoot.

The best time to kill a gobbler is nearly always the first real good shot which presents itself. The second or third shots are not usually as good as that first golden opportunity. What is a good shot? When does opportunity present itself?

When a gobbler is approaching you, be prepared and the questions will be answered fully. Get yourself ready mentally and physically before it is time to shoot. When the turkey is inside of twenty-five yards, you should kill him when you have the first clear shot at his head and neck. The gobbler should be standing straight up and standing still. Ideally, the gobbler's beak should be pointed either to the right or left of you when you shoot. A gobbler which has his beak pointed at you, or is walking, or is in a strut, does not present the best of targets.

Some people seem a bit confused about how to get their gun up. If you have been caught by surprise and the turkey is standing before you with your position being with gun in lap instead of being trained on the gobbler, then you have only one choice. Raise your gun, put the bead halfway between the gobbler's head and body along the center of his neck and pull the trigger. Do this quickly, but not hurriedly.

Ideally, pick a spot where the turkey is going to walk and have your gun trained on that spot. When a walking turkey or strutting turkey gets to the spot you have picked out, give a soft whistle. The gobbler will invariably straighten up, you make the inch or two of correction, and shoot. Please don't waste any time.

Caught by surprise, I shoot for the neck. When a gobbler walks in front of my gun, I shoot for the head.

"Shoot Now!"

As I said, the soft whistle will make them stand tall for a moment. But don't think you can whistle, watch them stand tall, and then raise your gun and shoot. You can raise your gun and shoot all in one motion. You can train your gun on an unsuspecting turkey, whistle, and then shoot. But you cannot whistle, raise your gun, and expect the turkey to present you with a good shot. The soft whistle, or even a smacking sound with your lips is a good tool to use, but only when you are looking down the barrel of your gun at a turkey which is totally unaware of your presence.

If the gobbler should duck his head and begin moving away from you, you must not shoot. More than half of these gobblers are lost to die some time later where you cannot retrieve them.

If the turkey is outside of thirty-five yards, you must not shoot no matter how clear a shot you have at the gobbler. I have never seen a shotgun which would kill a gobbler every time at thirty-five yards. I have seen only a few twelve gauges which would *not* kill them every time at thirty yards, and I have seen only a few guns of any gauge which would *not* kill them inside of twenty-four yards. Shots outside of forty yards are completely foolhardy. Even if you hit the gobbler at that range, it is a fluke if you damage his central nervous system enough to get him.

During the first week of this past season, I missed two gobblers at twenty and twenty-five yards, while hunting with a three inch twelve gauge. I missed them clean, did not touch a feather, because I did not fire at either one of them in a standing erect and standing still position. Both gobblers ducked away from my shot just as I fired. I guess I was feeling invincible with that big gun.

After switching to a .410 gauge, six shots collected six trophy gobblers. I killed them at ranges of 12, 15, 17, 19, 20, and 22 yards. Every one of them were standing stock still when I shot. Not a single one of the six gobblers even raised his head after I shot. The reason was simple—I knew that I had to make the proper shot with the little .410.

Small shot are much better for killing gobblers at close range. The small shot, however, do not retain much of their punch at ranges beyond thirty-five yards. Large shot retain their power all right, but few guns pattern the large shot well enough to hit that central nervous system with its vital organs of the head and neck. You must, I repeat, you must hit the gobbler in some part of the central nervous system if you expect to retrieve him.

If the right shot does not present itself, let me reiterate, don't shoot. You will eventually be sorry if you do. You might kill a gobbler or two which are trying to get away as you are about to shoot. These kinds of turkeys are always a mess if you do happen to get one every once in a while.

Some folks give themselves away about being poor turkey hunters by bringing these gobblers around for everyone to see. They will look like a busted feather pillow or something, with legs and wings all broken and askew. My dad once gave me a stern scolding for accidentally breaking a gobbler's leg while I was carrying the bird out of the woods. He said I needed to have a little more pride in what I was doing. Some of the members of our turkey hunting fraternity even groom their gobblers before bringing them in; one guy even washed a little spot of blood off his gobbler's head before coming out of the woods.

If you see some joker throw a dead gobbler down on the ground for examination, or jerk some feathers out of the bird, be leery of that person—he ain't no real turkey hunter. He doesn't have any respect for the bird and the fallen gobbler is just a hunk of dead meat to him.

Of course you can't make a dead turkey look pretty if he has been shot anywhere except the neck and head. I actually prefer for my tur-

".410 gauge is plenty gun; left pattern at 32 yards, right pattern at 24 yards—7½ sized shot."

keys to have more shot in their neck. They don't scoot along the ground so much if they have plenty of shot in the neck. I like the flopping the neck shot gives. The flopping is plenty violent and yet the turkey doesn't pull half his feathers out flipping around through the briars like he does if only hit in the head.

Saving Grace

You will be surprised at the good things which will occur if you do not shoot every gobbler which presents itself to be shot. On more than several occasions I have passed up shots at turkeys with nine inch beards, only to have gobblers with eleven and twelve inch beards show up a little while later. If you will practice this, not only will you be able to gather more trophy gobblers, but you will actually learn some things from the turkeys which you let go. A person who tries to kill as many turkeys as he can in a single day is without a doubt what is known as a slob hunter. He lacks self confidence or something. Our sport of turkey hunting should be above the meat hunting stage by now.

"Let this one go!"

"Same aged gobblers regroup late in the spring"

"Follow the Leader"

11 Master of Evasion and Escape

Any wild creature which manages to survive more than one year out there where they live must necessarily become masters in all phases at the game of evasion and escape. In the case of the wild turkey, much of this important behavior is *innate* or inborn into the turkey. The complex mechanism of *imprinting* in the young by the brood hen results in still other behavioral patterns which assist in survival. Still other characteristics of individuals within a flock are learned. Unique behavior is almost without exception, *learned*.

I have told the story many times of the captured baby turkey poults we put in a pen for raising several years ago. Some local kids caught them on the side of a country road; the poults were still in the downy stage. The kids presented the chicks to us like they had accomplished some worthwhile deed. We were unsuccessful in locating the hen from whence the little ones came.

We had a terrible time getting the little fellows to eat. We managed to get them to eat only by accident. Our daughter, Vicki, who was a small child at the time, had gathered a bunch of little bugs called "rolly-polies". These little critters of the centipede persuasion roll themselves into a little ball when handled. Vicki kept rolling the little bugs in front of the baby turkeys and finally one of the birds pecked, *instinctively*, at one of the rolly-polies. Somehow that act encouraged all of them to begin pecking and in a short while, the birds all began to eat.

Within three days, the youngsters were devouring several pounds of grasshoppers a day. At first, we hooked a piece of screen on the back of the truck and dragged the wire through a pasture to collect our insects. We hand fed each little turkey and they began to develop quickly.

We then rigged up a container holding live crickets and grasshoppers so that the insects could get out through a narrow passage which led straight to the pen housing the poults. Only one insect at a time could pass through the opening. I was surprised to see how fast the young birds *learned* to wait at the hole for the next unsuspecting insect attempting to make a getaway.

When the poults were less than eight days old, we put them in a big enclosure under the shade trees in our back yard. We could see them through the bathroom window without letting the birds be aware of our presence. An extension cord ran out there and was hooked up to a tape recorder. All kinds of sounds were played to the little turkeys and we observed their reactions. Most sounds didn't even interest them, but the recordings of alarm calls of a hen turkey brought dramatic results.

At the first note of alarm, the little fellows would scatter and freeze just as still as a rock. Every single time the recording of alarm notes was played, the poults reacted the same way. Some would be half under the leaves and others would just lay out flat on the ground. The little birds would come out of hiding after a little while; always in the same order. The little turkey we called Henry would invariably be the first to move and the last one to come out was always the one our daughter called Nelda. I tried a variety of calls to lure them out of hiding, but they paid no attention. More alarm calls would prolong their hiding freeze though. When they did come out of hiding, they would all emit a little buzzing racket, like a mini-purr; and then peep a little to each other.

This kind of scattering and freezing behavior is most assuredly *instinctive* since all of the little ones did it the same way each time without variation. The fact that some were half under the leaves was purely coincidental.

The behavior of the penned, wild hatched turkeys was consistent with the behavior of those I have observed in the wild. But a real brood hen can call her young out of hiding at her slightest command. After all, the wild hen calls almost constantly to her brood, beginning even before the poults are hatched. Wild hens make a couple of sounds, and the frequency, pitch, and rhythm of each hen probably has some *individual identity* to it which the young poults recognize.

Much of the behavior of turkeys is either instinctive or formed through *imprinting*. It is really fascinating to watch a flock of forty or more turkeys feeding on bahaia seed in late summer. The whole flock, every individual, will grasp the grass stalk in the same manner and give the same head pull and twist to gather in ninety percent of the seed on the stalk. These kinds of behavior are essential for survival of individuals and of the species.

No veteran turkey hunter can say that he has not encountered several wily gobblers or even hens which have shown some unique behavior of some kind. Learned behavior definitely helps the birds survive, especially as adult birds.

It is the *learned behavior* which is most interesting. The very unusual things which turkeys learn to do are what hold a special appeal for me. Since unique behavior among individuals is generally recognized as the learned type, we say that turkeys do indeed exhibit *intelligence* when they display the sort of action. When turkeys use learned behavior to survive, we might say they are *resourceful*. When an old gobbler uses learned maneuvers to escape a hunter, we say he is *slick* (among other unprintable terms).

At times we become so engrossed in whatever it is that a bird is doing, we forget all about killing these creatures and are satisfied to tell about how some turkey or another did something incredible to us. All hunters get a certain amount of satisfaction from being "out-foxed" by an old gobbler, whether he pulls a common stunt or unfolds a new trick we have never witnessed before.

I knew one old gobbler who lived in a little hollow behind a cemetery close back to a black-topped highway. Since the old bird had lived a long time and had gained somewhat of a reputation, I set in after him by first observing his movements in and around the country graveyard. He was a real character.

He paid no attention to calling instruments unless I was too close to him. If I did any calling within seventy-five yards of him, he would just move off a little ways and resume what he was already doing; he wouldn't even look in my direction.

At the sight of a real hen, the gobbler would immediately walk in a circle and then come to a full strut, always facing from right to left of the hen in question. If the hen did not come directly to him, he would break strut, walk in another circle, and strut some more. He never stayed in a strut for any long period of time before coming out and walking in that strange little circling maneuver of his.

Many years later, I learned why some old gobblers walk in that little circle. Turkeys which have trouble seeing out of one of their eyes due to injury or disease will employ the circle walking tactic to give themselves a full field of view.

When a car approached on the highway near the cemetery, the old gobbler would really show his stuff. If any other turkeys were in the field when a car approached, they would come to attention and watch closely until the car passed. If a car happened to stop, the turkeys would run into the woods. Not the old gobbler. At the sound of every single approaching vehicle, he would calmly walk behind a large thistle growing in the field and squat. When the car passed, he would stand up, adjust his feathers, and come out again.

He had a dusting hole within thirty feet of the highway which he used every day between ten and eleven o'clock, a period when there was very little traffic on the highway. If a car did happen by, the old tom would lay flat as a pancake in the dusting hole until the car was well past his spot.

He was a smart bird. The cemetery keeper finally cut the thistle down. Then the gobbler began to take cover behind a gas can which the keeper had left by a flower bush at the cemetery gate. I have seen other turkeys run behind objects to hide and I have seen a great many of them squat when danger approached. This character, though, planned his evasion tactics. He was well aware of the fact that if he wasn't seen by man, then he couldn't very well get shot.

It is well known about the *fake pecking behavior* of some turkeys. There are two separate uses for gobblers to lower their head and pretend to be pecking at grass blades and yet not really be catching or grasping anything but air.

The bent neck posture with the head held close to the ground is sometimes part of the male turkey's courtship ritual. Even while they are strutting, some gobblers will momentarily fake peck at the ground every once in a while. This behavior is similar to that of other bird species which offer a twig or grass blade to their prospective mates.

Mostly though, the old tom turkeys will deliberately pretend to lower their heads to peck for food and suddenly look up in the direction of suspected danger. I have even seen them lower their heads and go through the actual motion of pecking, but really all the time they are looking at the area where they expect danger. The *peek-a-boo* a second or third time from behind a tree is similar to this. That quick pulling back of the head by suspicious gobblers has saved many a turkey life from something or someone which might have been trying to get the drop on him. After all, predators, and man in particular, tries to move his position for a better vantage when he thinks the turkey is not looking or when the turkey has his vision obscured.

The *serpentine approach* of a gobbler coming to a caller has a two fold purpose. Many times I have seen gobblers coming to my calling with their heads barely three inches above the ground, their legs bent and their bodies held as close to the earth as possible. They will alter their course of approach to take advantage of every little bit of cover and any slight rise in the ground. This approach enables them to sneak up on hunters and in the same fashion, to sneak away from the would be shooter, completely undetected. I often wonder just how many countless gobbers have used this snake-like gait to get away none the worse for wear!

The nature of the wild gobbler is such that he does not want to be seen by anything except other turkeys. The snake-like slipping around in the woods allows the gobbler to also sneak up on those sometimes reluctant females and display before them quietly. It is the sight of the opposite sex in the proper pose which stimulates turkeys of both sexes to respond for the mating act. In areas where turkeys do not gobble much for one reason or another, the serpentine approach of the gobbler often allows the sexes to get together so the sultan can display before the females in all his glory before the hens sneak off from him for another year.

The standing erect posture of the alert wild turkey has much survival benefit about it. Nearly everything growing in the wild has a vertical or straight up and down look to it. An animal standing in the erect pose with its body lines pretty well straight up and down has a way of blending into its surroundings quite effectively. Some species of bitterns and herons are masters of this little game. The wild turkey can also become practically invisible right before your eyes.

I once saw a group of young hen turkeys run across a road into a thin strip of gum trees. When I got to the place where they just had to be, I could not see them at all for several minutes even though they were within thirty feet of my car. One of the young birds finally dropped its head and took a step. I then began seeing the other birds one at a time, standing quietly and calmly in the thicket.

Many older gobblers and hens seem to be in the erect and alert position ninety percent of the time. An approaching gobbler which suddenly stands erect and becomes stock still has a reason for doing this. He might have seen you and is trying to blend in and make a sneak out of there undetected. You will find that educated gobblers will take a slow measured step if this is the case—in the opposite direction of his original route. He may retrace his steps exactly. He will never bend his neck or jerk his head from side to side. The head jerking is a sign of panic. The tip of the old gobbler's tail will be pointed at the ground and the tip of his beak will be pointed skyward. His body lines will indeed be in a straight up and down plane.

If you look directly at him and make eye to eye contact, he will most likely duck his head and be away from there faster than light itself. Look at him out of the corner of your eye. The gobbler may continue to ease out of there ever so slowly. they can be some kind of sneaky.

Since the turkey can look at an object with only one eye at a time, this side to side head moving we see in turkeys helps the bird get an object triangulated for depth perception. Then the bird can tell more accurately just how far away the danger is.

Also, the rods and cones in birds' eyes are located in clusters on different parts of the retina. The tilting of the head, which we see in turkeys as well as other species of birds, allows light to strike all parts of the retina and thus activates rods and cones thoroughly. Better color perception and light gathering qualities occur, enabling the bird to take a clearer more vivid picture of that danger which may be lurking nearby.

Knowing this, imagine how hard it must be for a wise old gobbler to keep his head so very still with these slow deliberate sneak away movements. If the old bird before you makes a few feet of headway at getting away undetected, one can literally see his confidence build. Don't think he is not ready though. If one moves and points his weapon at the same time, the hunter might have two tenths of one second to get the drop on him. If the gobbler ducks and darts away when you make your move, don't shoot. Turkeys which panic are often shot in the butt by turkey hunters who panic. No gobbler deserves to be shot in the rear end. Let him go.

Of course the head with all the colors of spring passion is the most conspicuous part of a turkey gobbler. The instantly reacting nervous system allows the gobbler to change the bright red, white and blue into sort of a dull ash gray color within a few short seconds. This also helps the turkey blend in with his cover.

No one argues that wild turkeys would rather run from danger than to fly from it. In particular, the proper response to man is for the turkey to duck, run a short ways, and then if man is close or still in sight, to fly off. Since escaping turkeys, who live long enough to learn, have often been shot at or even peppered on their take off, sometimes it becomes impossible to make one fly at all. If you happen up on a turkey which seems reluctant to fly, chances that the bird has had more than one bad experience with stalking types of hunters are real high.

A gobbler which has become hesitant about flying is a very shy secretive, and retiring critter. They may not leave an area, but they will often quit all gobbling if they are repeatedly spooked and become almost impossible to hunt effectively by calling.

I was once after a big tom which stayed in a one hundred acre island of woods in the middle of a large pasture. I didn't do a real good job of hunting and managed to scare him several times. A couple of other hunters were also after the turkey; they had even fired at him on two separate occasions. One day the other fellows, unknown to me, were sitting on the east side of the woods where they spooked the turkey out of there. The bird left on a dead run heading north along the edge of the woods. I just happened to be coming up on the west side of the island when I spotted the turkey coming around the north edge of the woods. I froze and the turkey ran on past me, heading south. A few minutes later, the two men came walking out of the woods leaving the area. They told me what had happened and left. I just plopped down on the ground to think about the situation and try to figure out where I might go looking for another gobbler.

In less than ten minutes, I spotted the gobbler retracing his steps from the earlier run he had made. He pecked a little bit in the pasture and then went into the woods at the exact spot from whence the two hunters had appeared only a few minutes before. Throughout the remainder of the season, the gobbler was seen around the island of woods. He quit gobbling, but he most certainly did not go anywhere. He survived the hunting season.

The following season, the gobbler was again hanging out around the island of woods. The bird gobbled plenty prior to the opening of the season, but ceased all gobbling soon thereafter. He was shot at and missed again by yet another hunter. In all, over a period of three hunting seasons, eight different turkey hunters gave chase to this gobbler. No one ever saw him fly until a young fellow saw him sail down from his roost one morning. Maybe this is an extreme example of a turkey becoming strictly a ground bird, but I can assure you that human encounters assist them in becoming very much like a roadrunner.

Many old gobblers have unusual ways which enable them to stay alive by evading and escaping when danger threatens. One of the finest gobblers I ever hunted, gobbled only when he was way out in the middle of a field. The bird would spend most of the day out of harms way in the very center of a big opening. When he left the field, he would take off running and fly way over the top of the timber, landing a quarter of a mile or so back in the woods. He also arrived in the field by air mail. Apparently this gobbler realized that field edges are good places to get shot during the open turkey season and was going to huge extremes to avoid getting ambushed.

I zapped him after three years of hunting by waiting out in the middle of the field. I lay flat on my back for three hours before he gyrated up to my calling, just gobbling and strutting like crazy. You might imagine how uncomfortable I was, not being able to see more than thirty yards. I did have the presence of mind not to shoot my toe off when the bird finally arrived on top of me.

Some of the Cassanova types of longbeards use their entourage to alert them to the first hint of danger. One gobbler I remember had half a dozen hens come to his gobbling every morning. When a mating was about to take place, the other hens and the pair of jakes which hung around would form a loose circle around the pair of mating turkeys. There was no way for anything or anyone to sneak up on the turkeys while the intimate business was going on. The *sentinels* (lookouts) kept a sharp watch as the group traveled from one place to another.

One morning I called this Cassanova and the whole group to me. As they approached my position, the birds divided into two groups. First the two jakes and a large hen approached, while the remainder of the troupe stayed behind, well out of shotgun range. The gobbler stayed in full strut while the investigating team looked the situation over. The eventualPutt! Putt! of alarm came from the hen and the whole crowd left the scene in a hurry.

On the subject of sentinels or lookouts, the intricate role they play in flock behavior and survival is fascinating. Some members of a flock can sound an alarm call and the rest of the flock doesn't react too drastically. But let one of several selected hens in a flock make even a single note of alarm and the whole flock will instantly react and take the correct evasion actions necessary. These trusted sentinels are usually large old hens.

The greatest turkey I ever knew was named Spooky and the two old hens who stayed by his side from February until they laid their eggs in April were even more alert than he was. During the time of year (June through mid February) when the brood hens and the young of the year remain together, every turkey within two square miles of their range looked to those two old gals for guidance and direction.

It is said that turkeys do not know what a shotgun noise is all about. Bull! One October morning, I shot a squirrel at first light. Unknown to me, there was a large flock of turkeys roosting within a hundred yards of the hickory where the squirrels fed. At the sound of the shot, the two old Spooky hens lit about sixty yards away and set up such a chorus of clucking and loud yelping and all kinds of noises like you never heard. No other turkeys made a sound, but in less than three minutes, there were thirty-five turkeys standing over there with the old hens.

By some unseen cue or unheard signal, they arranged themselves in single file; the two hens stationed one at each end of the column. The lead hen then led the whole procession past me, coming at the closest point over the top of a small knob on the ridge across the hollow from where I was standing. When each turkey stepped up on the knob, one at a time, each turkey would emit a single sharp cluck just like the turkey before it, and then proceed on down the ridge in the procession. When the old rear guard hen, the last in line, stepped up, she paused for about ten seconds. She gave me a real thorough going over. She walked off and returned four times without making a sound. Finally, she let out a series of sharp cutts and left for good, clucking loudly every once in a while as she caught up with the exiting column. the whole tribe broke into a trot and left the area, looking like a line of soliders on a forced march. The flock did not roost there again for a month. It was a beautiful thing to see how the two old hens not only looked out for the young flock, but educated them to the identity of man the hunter as well.

Once a young physics student of mine and I were pursuing an old tom which roosted every night about three hundred yards off a gravel road. Every morning we would drive over there and worry the turkey until we had to leave for school at seven o'clock. The gobbler would gobble plenty, but would not fly down off his roost. I tried everything

I knew of to get him down from there, including not calling at all. After five straight mornings of attempts, we had not succeeded. The student suggested that the turkey might be hearing us drive up in my volkswagon on the gravel road. I told him that turkeys were used to hearing cars on the road and that didn't have anything to do with it. Being from downtown New Orleans, the boy didn't know a thing about turkeys. He had yet to see his first wild turkey since he had only recently moved to our little rural community.

On the sixth morning, just to appease the boy, I instructed the kid to drive the car on down the road and come back and get me at seven o'clock. The boy left me and the gobbling turkey at six forty-five and walked out to the road and cranked up the volkswagon. I could hear it plainly from where I sat listening to the gobbling turkey. No sooner had he driven out of hearing than the turkey flew down and walked straight to my calling. About the time the turkey quit flopping, I heard the volkswagon coming back. The boy finally got to see a real wild turkey, even though it was a dead one.

That kid sure had a good time in physics class for a couple of weeks, telling faculty and fellow students alike how he had figured out how to kill a wise old gobbler with an eleven and one half inch beard.

Survival may begin with instinct, but it ends with learned behavior. Shotguns are a different kind of predator which instinct does not deal with too effectively. I don't reckon it really matters what design enables gobblers to get away so often. The fact that they can evade and escape so regularly is what captures our fancy.

"One may breed"

12 The Preferred Male

Since 1956, I have made literally thousands of casual observations of the wild turkey in its natural surroundings. I have compiled many pages of notes and logged many journals on what I have observed. Since no study of any wild creature can be all revealing, especially those little two year long jobs done by our fledgling biologists, please accept the following for what it is; my own personal testimony to what I believe is the truth concerning the very existence of the species, the eastern wild turkey.

Laymen's terms are used in the passage so that the most frequent reader, the turkey hunter, can glean the maximum amount of information from these few short pages of summary from a lifetime of observation and study of that special wild turkey—the preferred male.

I have been afforded the opportunities to observe at great length my favorite subject and the implications I make about my own personal stomping grounds in this part of the world known as the "Florida Parishes" in our great state of Louisiana are well intended. Every hunter of any worth considers his home territory as special. With our case, the private lands around here have been a blessing to me and to the wild turkey. Without them, I could not have enjoyed my forty years here on earth (to date) nearly as fully.

Back to the preferred male—no photograph does him justice and no written word is entirely accurate. He is above all other wild things. While it is true that he exhibits all the personalities and traits described here and in other writings, he is a cut above. He is the reason the wild turkey exists as a species. I will attempt to explain what he is as best I can, and how to deal with him in a sporting manner.

To say that the preferred male wild gobbler deserves a chapter all his own would be a tremendous understatement. He needs several volumes for himself. He is that important. I will, however, deal with him only briefly here. If you hunt turkeys very long, you will make your own summaries anyway and I have not yet found two people who see him in exactly the same light.

A *preferred male turkey* is one which has come to be favored by more than one or two females of the species within a given stretch of woods. How this comes about, I do not know. I used to think it had to do with the way some males gobble. Then I began to think it was the way some of them displayed or strutted before their captive female audiences. Now I say that I do not have a clue as to the reason they are so much more attractive to the hen turkeys than the other male turkeys in their areas.

Some biologists will suggest that the peck order, the ranking system, or power alignment within a flock, determines which gobblers will be selected as the most prolific breeders. Some claim that the most dominant gobblers are the ones occupying the status of breeding males. I will agree that often the most aggressive gobblers are those which are also preferred for breeding by the hen flock, but I can cite many instances where preferred gobblers were not the dominant gobblers of the area. Sometimes, a lesser gobbler is the preferred mating partner of many hens within the locale of a super dominant gobbler who hardly gains the favor of but a few hens.

I do know that these preferred males control the breeding activities of the area they occupy, whatever the reason. At this latitude, these preferred turkey gobblers have the uncanny wit to be in the company of a group of hens from mid February until mid April. These gobblers show much stronger territorial behavior patterns than other gobblers and do set up sort of a generalized daily routine or pattern.

These daily routines unfold according to the season. If it is early in March (here), his routine on good weather days is occupied with the following of a large number of hens around through their feeding grounds. He usually gobbles a little from his roosting tree which is normally close to the roosting flock of hens and sometimes younger gobblers. Hens, as you might expect, gravitate to his gobbling, and he flies down near the first arriving females; he struts and breeds the first hen to show the proper response by crouching before him. The bred hen shakes herself and moves away towards the feeding grounds. Traveling as a flock, many hens will become "struck" by his display during the day, and the old boy will respond properly every time. Twenty or more hens may be in the flock and he will follow them around all day. Depending upon food supply, the gobbler and his flock of hens may travel several miles per day, often traveling in a big circle or oval pattern through the turkey woods. I have observed this phenomenon during the first two weeks of March over two hundred times with at least one hundred and twenty-five different gobblers and hen flocks.

There may be more than one gobbler within the intact group of hens, but my persistent surveillance has only witnessed one gobbler to be the preferred breeding tom. Any gobbler with lofty social status may strut, but on no occasion have I ever seen more than one gobbler to have actually bred a hen while in the company of the still intact hen flock.

If bad weather occurs during this early spring breeding time, which may begin in February, the routine of the gobbler and flock is altered only to the extent that less gobbling is done. The preferred male may take a day or two out of his routine to preen and oil himself during rainy weather, but then he gets right back to the business at hand. He does less gobbling during bad weather, but does not let weather interfere with his breeding. During the first week of March in 1975, I saw a gobbler mate with 14 different hens during a six hour period. It rained all day.

As spring progresses, the "busting up" of flocks will occur. Within the territory of the chosen gobbler, there may be only a few hens still roosting close to the gobbler. Many of the original flock may be as far as five miles away, getting themselves ready to prepare a clutch of eggs. Until actual incubation of the eggs begins, the hens will continue to visit the preferred gobbler no matter how far away he is. The hens do not come every day and the later and closer to incubation (setting) time it becomes, the more sporadic and less frequent will be their visits. The preferred gobbler accomplishes "visiting hours" by establishing a strutting zone or "display area" on or very near the favorite feeding grounds of the hens which have stayed close to his roosting area.

Now the gobbler does more gobbling from the roost before he flies down. (If he has not been disturbed on his roost.) If a hen arrives, he flies down early. If no hens arrive early at the roost tree, the gobbler spends more time on the roost gobbling and then he flies down.

He then marches to a prescribed display area and begins to gobble more and more. Sooner or later hens begin to arrive. He may or may not breed them. Sometimes the distant arrivals are bred and sometimes they do not respond properly for mating to occur. The visiting hens go and come all during the morning hours to the gobbler's display area for several weeks, maybe as long as a month. I have seen as many as six hens become bred at these display areas within a single morning, and the most hens that I ever saw visit a display area during a single morning was during the last week of March in 1964; fifteen hens came on that morning, singularly and in groups of two or three.

Sometime (late March-early April) during the late morning hours, the gobbler's mood will change; he will fix his wings just so over his back and he will march straight to water, with or without hens. He soon returns to the display area and seeks out those hens which have roosted close to him. Those hens which visited him from afar have long gone. When the gobbler gets in the company of those half a dozen or so hens which are laying close by, he will fix himself in a full round strut and follow them as long as he can. If he can stay with them all day, he will. Shortly before roosting time he will separate himself from them a short ways. After he goes to roost, he will often gobble a few times just to let the hens close by know where he is.

If the hens slip away from the gobbler during the day, he will often frantically try to gobble them up just before sundown. He calls urgently when his close contingent is not present in the afternoon. At other times he will try to rendezvous with them in some favorite feeding place. I have seen some wait quietly until the little group of hens makes their appearance and then if the bird is not satisfied with the small number of hens he may encounter, gobble incessantly with a couple of hens right next to him.

Sometimes, the preferred gobbler comes in contact with a more dominant gobbler in the peck order. The preferred one will usually retire from the presence of the dominant turkey to avoid combat. He does little or no strutting in the company of the dominant bird. Invariably, the more dominant gobbler will leave the area on his own accord after a little while, and the preferred gobbler will resume his activities as though nothing happened. Please keep in mind that the preferred gobbler often is the most dominant gobbler. In fact, some of them become dominant because the more dominant ones get killed by hunters.

The described early season and late season routines of breeding gobblers is pretty consistent, but to say that they always establish a set pattern would not be entirely accurate. As I said, they may exhibit a number of different personalities known to turkeys. A circuit riding type of preferred male does tend to ride the same circuit for weeks at a time. The circuit rider may spend several hours at each display zone, or he may spend several days at each area. A suspicious gobbler may not gobble for days at a time, but you can bet that he will be strutting before his hens somewhere. A reclusive gobbler will tend to set up on the same forty acre plot of woods and do his thing for days and days.

Barring serious disturbances, the preferred gobbler actively seeks out and encourages hens to mate for the entire season, or so long as his gonads are swollen and the mating desire has a hold of him. There is really not a lot of variation in the preferred gobbler's behavior. That's just the way they act.

This brings us to an important question. How does the hunter deal with the Cassanova gobblers who are almost always in the company of hens? They are a lot of fun to hunt, but they are very difficult to kill by sporting means. You might kill them regularly by ambushing them at food plots or over bait when they follow their hens around. They will challenge the best hunter in fair chase situations though.

I have had good luck by getting close to the display areas and calling softly and periodically. It is best to answer a gobbler of this sort rather than trying to make him answer you. You see, if he isn't gobbling, you can bet that he is very busy at the moment. He is also vulnerable to calling when he is returning from water late in the mornings. He is actually looking for and seeking out hens at this time. The preferred gobbler will also come to a call (sometimes) just after he has parted from his company before going to roost late in the afternoon.

Back on the subject of display areas, you must remember to be extremely careful with your movements in and around these places. You can get into these areas to call at the gobbler, but you must be very careful; this is a familiar place to the turkey. Imagine some joker marching up in your bedroom and catching you by surprise. It would be equally, if not more, unnerving to the turkey gobbler, if not for the same reasons.

Here are some eye witness accounts which point out the validity of what I have offered about the behavior of the special male turkeys.

The ability of these males to actually command an audience of a flock of hens is amazing. Once I observed a white hen with a loose feather on her head go to roost in a magnolia tree. *I saw her*. The next morning I was calling a preferred gobbler two miles from that magnolia tree. The gobbler was in his display area gobbling and strutting. He had a couple of hens to visit him early. At 7:45, the white hen with the loose feather on her head showed up. The gobbler strutted around and around her in circles. She crouched and he climbed upon her and mating occurred. The white hen vigorously shook herself and left. The turkey gobbled a couple of times and several other hens arrived. At ten o'clock the gobbler left the area, but he was back within thirty minutes. A little more gobbling took place and three hens showed up, the white hen was not among them. The preferred gobbler of this area began to strut furiously and left following the three hens, none of which showed the slightest interest in him, even though they did arrive at his gobbling.

For five straight mornings I watched the gobbler arrive in the display area and do his thing with lots of gobbling and strutting. I did not see the white hen again until that fifth morning. I could see the gobbler at all times during the mornings that I was in there after him. The hens of a flock do not visit a single particular preferred gobbler every day after egg laying begins.

Several years back, some two weeks before the hunting season was to begin, Ben Jones of Baton Rouge called and asked if I knew where he might go hear and see some turkeys. I had been observing several big gobblers, one of them a preferred male, for a few days. I directed Ben to that spot.

Ben observed a hen approaching a gobbling turkey at daylight. The gobbler flew to the hen and the hen began assembly yelping. In a very short period of time a convoy of turkeys headed up a log road and into an open area where the turkeys habitually fed during the morning hours. Ben observed several mature gobblers strutting among the flock of hens, but only one gobbler did any breeding. Ben was in the hiking mood and he lit out on a long walk through several miles of beautiful woods which were full of turkeys. He saw no more turkeys, heard none gobble, and reported in his words, "All the action was in one place".

One week later, the atmosphere had changed—literally. The season opened in yet another week and Bob Price of our turkey hunting fraternity went with me into the area after gobblers. I was on a beautiful hardwood ridge where the visibility was about one hundred and fifty yards. Bob had taken a position about four hundred yards from me. At daylight, five mature gobblers began to talk. One big gobbler flew down about a hundred yards north of where I was waiting. Soon three hens walked past the big gobbler which was making a lot of noise with his gobbling. The hens made their way on to the east where the preferred gobbler was gobbling periodically. I called the gobbler which was close to me and after about an hour, he strolled up to me and I shot him at a range of about twenty yards. I returned to where Bob was stationed and put my gobbler in a tree stand.

Bob and I started in the direction of the preferred gobbler's display area. When we arrived the turkey had ceased gobbling for the moment. We stopped just over a hill from where the tom just had to be. After a pretty good wait, the gobbler advertised again and I called back to him with a three note quaver of a young hen. The preferred gobbler stalked up to within twenty steps of Bob and me, but since Bob could not get a clear shot at him, we let the turkey walk off. We left soon after our aborted attempt for that day.

That gobbler stayed within a forty acre stretch of woods for three weeks. His routine stayed the same day after day. He was a fine specimen, and we named him the "Main Most Turkey". His pattern involved going to water at a man made slough every morning around 10:30. His display area remained the same and hens visited him every day. We did not ever come close to fooling the turkey again; he is still over there.

Here is another experience which is typical of spring time behavior. The setting was thus: a large creek had a preferred male on each side of its banks. The male on the east side of the creek was the dominant bird, a three year old gobbler. The turkey on the west side of the creek was a two year old bird. Every morning both of these turkeys had hens visit them in their respective display areas. About every third day, the three year old gobbler would cross the creek and whip up on the two year old gobbler.

The next day the two year old gobbler would be at it again, and his hens would pay him a visit. Four hens visited the gobbler on the west bank nearly every morning. The east bank gobbler had a large number of hens around him all the time.

About three-fourths of a mile north of these gobblers, an old gobbler sang to the world every morning. No hens were ever observed in his company. Several jakes used the area and would gobble on good ideal gobbling mornings. The three year old gobbler chased them all around too.

The very old gobbler was killed by a hunter who called him up after a two hour calling session. The three year old gobbler was missed twice by another hunter who gobbled at the turkey. The bird quit gobbling, but his hens continued to visit him at the strutting zone for several weeks. The two year old gobbler would not leave the immediate vicinity of his display area, and would not respond to any kind of calling. He did not receive any lead for his trouble and stayed put in that area for years. I never learned what became of the three year old dominant gobbler after the year that I observed him.

Here are some points of interest about hunting these kinds of gobblers:

1. Dominant gobblers are sometimes also preferred gobblers.
2. Preferred gobblers which are not dominant will give ground to dominant birds, but will resume their breeding activities when the dominant bird is not present.
3. Preferred gobblers which are not dominant gobblers tend to be reclusive and stick to the same locale.
4. Dominant gobblers which are also preferred gobblers often take on the Vagabond or Circuit Riding personality.
5. Movements in and around display zones should be undertaken with extreme caution.
6. Circuit riding gobblers will usually announce their presence when they arrive at each successive display area by gobbling.
7. Preferred gobblers are most vulnerable to calling when they are returning from water without hens, when they have left their hens to go to roost, and when they have been separated from the hens they are following. Sometimes they can be called directly off the roost by imitating flying down sounds of a hen.
8. Hens of a flock do not visit a gobbler every day after egg laying begins. The later in the season, the more sporadic are the visits from hens and the more anxious gobblers become. Ninety percent of the preferred gobblers which are killed by hunters in a sporting (calling) manner are killed during the late part of a season.
9. Bad weather affects gobbling, but not breeding to any real degree.

Disturbances by humans may alter a turkey's routine, but will not deter him from seeking out and breeding hens.
10. A preferred gobbler following hens will often lag behind at likely ambush points. His advance guard keeps a sharp lookout for danger. It seems that somehow these special toms know of their importance and the other members of the flock comprehend also.
11. A preferred gobbler and/or a dominant gobbler will tolerate jakes in the area if they show no interest in breeding and make no threatening gestures. The preferred one acts like the jakes aren't even around. Very old gobblers are less tolerant of other gobblers than younger ones.
12. In areas where the preferred gobbler is also the dominant gobbler, the hunting and gobbling is usually good for that area. The preferred one is usually only concerned about what is going on really close to him.
13. The younger hens of a flock hang together as a roosting unit longer during the laying season. They are often the little group of "resident" hens which are close to a preferred gobbler. As the spring progresses, these little groups disassemble early in the mornings and regroup in the late afternoons.

The preferred male is an interesting product of a species which is capable of exhibiting strong reproductive capacity. The design by which breeding is ensured in the species is fascinating. Although many males in a population will and do breed on occasion, it is the selected few which breed the majority of the hens come rain or shine in the spring of the year. These birds never cease to amaze me. We see very little genetically inferior qualities in our turkey flocks and I cannot help but believe that this preferred male phenomenon has a lot to do with the fact that even these small gene pools turn out quite vigorous individuals and genetically sound flocks.

PART THREE

Management of Turkeys and People

"A clutch of turkey eggs"

13 Put Something Back

The wild turkey has made a wonderful comeback. They are indeed restored to many parts of their range all over this continent. Huntable populations exist all over this great country. Turkey hunting mania is at a fever pitch. Today's sportsmen are reaping the benefits of those who have labored long and hard to bring about the return of the wild turkey since the pitiful existence of the few surviving flocks during the early part of this century.

However, the changing environment will someday be totally and irrevocably unsuitable for the wild turkey. Unless mankind precedes the birds in extinction, we probably will not be hunting turkeys for too much longer. That's not a very rosy picture, is it?

The future of the wild turkey will rest upon the actions of the modern day sportsmen. There are a number of things which must be done in order to prolong the turkey's stay here on earth. We must do what we can to conserve what we have now. We must throw up our fortifications in every effort to change the modern day trend of taking away the wild turkey's habitat for other forms of land use. There are some simple steps we can take to enhance the plight of our present populations.

In all populations, there are numerous forces which work against a species. Of course, the reproductive capacity of a species works for that species. Since this capacity of the wild turkey is strong and fairly constant, our time should be spent to negate the limiting forces which act against our populations of wild turkeys.

For the purpose of this discussion, I will place these limiting factors into five categories. These categories will be: 1) hunting, 2) habitat, 3) predation, 4) weather, and 5) disease. I will offer some advice on how to deal with each of these topics. I hope to show how all the limiting forces can be minimized by correcting attitudes and policies.

Hunting

Quite simply, the serious decline of the wild turkey which occurred during the first half of this century was caused by overhunting, or more correctly, the *over-killing* of turkeys. The market hunter killed many tens of thousands of the birds in his venture to feed an expanding urban human population. The family meat provider in rural America eliminated entire flocks of turkeys as our country expanded to every corner of the continent in terms of human numbers. Even the so called sportsmen of that era continued to hunt and kill all manner of turkeys while these same sportsmen clamored for protection and restoration measures.

We now have restrictive regulations which govern our hunting activities. Wanton killing of large numbers of turkeys by any one individual is pretty much a thing of the past. The question remains, however, whether these new conservation minded laws are enough. Albeit that our laws have teeth now. And our hunting public is much more conservation minded than during our early days when the average American felt that there was no end to our bounty.

Illegal hunting and poaching still remain a problem. We need to alert our local game wardens to the illegal hunting that we may know about. The law enforcement agencies everywhere need our help. We must ostracize and shun those who engage in unsavory and illegal hunting practices. We have no need of the few misfits among the modern day sportsmen.

We all need to exercise some self-restraint when it comes to killing wild turkeys. Staying within the limits of the law is not enough. Why, if every licensed hunter in the United States killed a wild turkey this year, the bird would vanish almost overnight. Thank goodness all of us don't pursue the wild turkey.

Within the little groups which do hunt turkeys, we need to place a few restrictive measures upon ourselves which surpass the legal standards. Here are a couple of policies practiced by the group which I hunt with:

1) We don't kill young gobblers.

2) We leave at least one mature gobbler per section (640 acres) of land upon which we hunt.

No biologist knows for sure how many male turkeys are necessary to sustain a thriving turkey population. We feel that even legal gobblers can be overkilled in an area.

Statistically, the younger birds make up the largest portion of all turkey flocks. By hunting only the older male birds, and by leaving at least one mature gobbler per section of land, we actually hunt only a very small percentage of the turkey population. Since we are looking for the old longbearded toms, the accidental shooting of hens is nonexistent. Our group assures itself of having quality trophy hunting year in and year out. The limiting factor we place on a flock of turkeys is insignificant. We don't overkill and we try desperately to have a good time. We have long since decided that hunting for a turkey to bake in an oven is an archaic practice. Each hunt is a recreational experience which we savor for years to come.

Examine the following hypothetical situation. It is purely an exercise in mathematics. Suppose that you and your neighbor own two sections of land between you. You have decided to adopt one of two policies available to you for harvesting gobblers. One policy will allow each of you to kill three gobblers per season; that is the legal limit in Louisiana. The alternate policy involves an agreement between you and your neighbor to leave one mature gobbler on each of the two sections of land, and not to kill any jakes (young gobblers) at all. The 1280 acres of land is good habitat.

For the purpose of this exercise, we will say that you had varying success in raising gobblers. For four years, the nesting success on the property varied, naturally, according to the following hypothetical data:

Best year	= 10 jakes
Worst year	= 2 jakes
Good year	= 7 jakes
Poor year	= 5 jakes

This means that you could have produced twenty four (24) jakes in four years.

If we assume that there was no mortality among the turkeys except for hunting by you, then by adopting a legal hunting harvest method, you and your neighbor could have *legally killed every single gobbler on the 1280 acres.* By practicing the alternate policy of not killing any young gobblers and by leaving a mature gobbler on each of the two sections, you could have harvested thirteen (13) long-bearded gobblers. You would theoretically have eleven (11) long-bearded birds left on the land to begin the fifth hunting season.

Of course this is a hypothetical situation. It would be impossible to keep all the turkeys you and your neighbor could raise on two square miles of prime turkey habitat. But if this restrictive harvesting policy were instituted on any real piece of good turkey habitat, I would guarantee the very real results of:

1) More turkeys per square mile.
2) More gobblers per square mile.
3) More trophy gobblers per square mile.
4) More gobbling activity on crisp spring mornings.

In 1975, I instituted such a harvest program on two thousand acres of land upon which I control the turkey hunting. Although we got no cooperation from our neighbors who allowed unrestrictive hunting, we have had good results with the program. Everyone who has hunted on this two thousand acre tract of land is impressed with the aggressive nature of the gobblers. We have an abundance of turkeys and since 1976, we have harvested nearly one hundred (100) long-bearded gobblers. Some of these trophies have qualified for the Louisiana record book for turkey spurs. As of this writing, May 1986, following our annual spring season, mind you, there are one dozen (12) gobblers on the 2000 acres with beards longer than ten inches. These are just the ones I know about. I observe this dozen regularly.

Our neighbors have also benefited. For miles around the tract of land we hunt on, there has been a great increase in the turkey population. There are literally hundreds of turkeys where there used to be only a few.

The restrictive harvesting policy is only a part of what has brought about these results.

Not too long ago, I had a man tell me about the success of his hunting club which was located in the southeastern part of this state. He informed that his group had killed four adult gobblers and four jakes on their lease during the 1986 season. I asked him why they killed the jakes. He told me that they had to keep ahead of some guy who was hunting to the south of them. He was also skeptical of the hunting group who used the land north of his.

It does not change things if someone is hunting in your neighborhood of turkey woods. Anyone who practices restrictive hunting does not only help himself, but those around him too. Every young gobbler you do not pull the trigger on still has a chance for survival. Even if the jake you pass up has only a fifty percent (50%) chance of escaping your neighbors' shotguns, that's better than you killing the bird. If you shoot and kill, then it's all over and the bird has zero chance of growing into a trophy gobbler. Shooting jakes does nothing except deprive hunters of recreational experiences. And recreational experiences are the only real worth of turkey hunting anyway.

Throughout the text of this book, you will find the terms; hunting group, hunting fraternity, hunting club, etc. In fact the last chapter in this book was put together by such a group. These groups are made up of guys all over the country who pay the freight for the existence of wild game for hunting. Since public lands are fast becoming prime places, along with war zones and international airports, for getting shot and killed, private leases are apt to be more and more popular among hunters.

I know that hunting is expensive for decent law abiding folks, and it's going to become even more costly to hunt in the future. When you begin to despair over all those hunting expenses, just compare the costs of your hunting endeavors with the costs of other kinds of recreation. Think of the cost of a single trip to some amusement center like Disney World.

Why my little family of three, plus a couple of neighborhood kids, managed to spend over a thousand dollars on a weekend trip to Houston just to see a couple of baseball games and to walk around in Astroworld for a little while. We wanted to see Nolan Ryan strike out the history making batter. The money we spent was hard earned, but we wanted to go, so we didn't really mind spending the money. Of course we don't go to Houston every weekend.

The bottom line is very easy to see. Turkey habitat is going to be placed into some other form of land use if hunting activities cannot pay their way.

Some years ago, I pursued a real fine old gobbler up and down a certain hardwood ridge north of town. I had a ball and did finally manage to get a good shot at my trophy gobbler. There were several flocks of turkeys using that area, and for years, that piece of property provided some fine recreational moments for a number of hunters. The owner of the property was approached by a real estate developer and was paid a handsome price for the land. Now some fifty or so houses have been built in there, one house full of kids located on the very spot where the birds once liked to roost. I'm afraid that habitat is gone forever.

If private landowners can realize some profit from their land being used for hunting, they are much more likely to keep their land suitable for game to use. The more profitable hunting becomes, the more serious the folks are going to become about making their land attractive and better habitat for all kinds of wildlife, including the wild turkey.

We can also attempt to have the landowners become more aware of the wildlife on their property so that maybe we can help them develop a sense of pride in those wild things which inhabit their land. I believe the majority of land owners have this sense of pride already. It just needs to be cultivated a little more and sort of encouraged, if you know what I mean. We need to make the owners aware of how important wildlife is to everyone.

Habitat

The habitat upon which turkey flocks depend for survival is extremely important. You can practice all the restrictive harvesting you want on land which will not sustain a flock of turkeys and you will never gain any ground. Any habitat, though, can be improved by human manipulations just as easily as it can be destroyed by the intervention of man.

Marginal habitat is that which barely fills the needs of the flock. *Ideal habitat* is that upon which turkey flocks and populations can actually thrive. *Preferred habitat* is that upon which turkeys spend more time than other parts of the terrain.

The changes you make within the environment can change marginal habitat into ideal habitat. Preferred areas may even be created. Here are some tips on what turkeys need and how they prefer to have the essentials presented to them.

Water is the first requirement which habitat must provide. Turkeys cannot do without a permanent source of water. Even though there are a few days when a turkey flock will absorb enough water from their food and may not actually drink water, the birds do have to have some permanent water to sustain them. Water drinking by turkeys is pretty doggone regular.

Running streams are ideal sources of water. The great linear distance of available water afforded by a stream makes more water accessible than a localized source such as a pond or a slough. The birds will naturally utilize ponds and sloughs where they are handy.

Ideally, water should be accessible within one fourth of a mile from any point on the terrain. The location of permanent water sources scattered throughout the habitat is preferred. Nesting activities take place within an easy walk from permanent water. Having the water sources scattered within the nesting cover will assure wide dispersal of the nesting flock throughout the habitat. Having the hens widely dispersed for their nesting activities has obvious survival benefits.

If ponds or sloughs are utilized by turkeys, disturbances at these locations should be kept at a minimum. Repeated disturbances at a localized source of water may cause turkeys to quit using that watering site eventually. That's almost as bad as having no water at all. Turkeys prefer to drink in areas which are free from thick undergrowth. Keep man-made watering sites free from undergrowth and with a clean area for easy access.

Turkeys will and do eat a large variety of different plant and animal foods. The plant foods make up the larger share of their diets. The ideal habitat provides an abundance of food which is easy to get to. Turkeys obtain their food from three basic areas within the habitat: 1) the woodlands, 2) the edges, 3) the open areas.

The woodlands would rank first in importance for providing food since our birds spend most of their time in the woods. As with water sources, the more woodland food sources, the better. Turkeys prefer to feed in woods which have very little understory of ground cover. Thick undergrowth sometimes prevents turkeys from fully utilizing food which may be present in the thick areas. Mast producing trees of good quality and vigor should be present in the turkey woods. A high percentage of trees should contribute to producing food. Some non-producing trees can be helpful in shading out the understory to make those "park-like" stands which turkeys prefer. In general turkey woods ideally are heavy to species with broad leaves. The oak-hickory type of hardwood stand is good. A stand which has a high percentage of oak species is very acceptable.

The cherrybark red oak, *Quercus falcata pagoda*, is a beautiful tree. These deep woods specimens have long clear boles (trunks) which are relatively free of knots and blemishes. The tree has a crown which occupies about one third of the area of the total tree. Notice how the specimen shades out the lesser trees around it. An acre of ground can sustain about forty of this sized tree (twenty eight inches in diameter) and this species does not "degrade" like some hardwood species, living quite vigorously until it is sixty or seventy years of age. That's a lot of years of acorn production. Forty of this sized trees per acre will have a total of about 12,000 board feet (doyle scale). At $150 per M, that's $1800 per acre worth of timber. Plant some of these and watch your wildlife and pocketbooks grow.

Photos from "Redwood Ranch" at Wilson, La., on the estate of the late J. T. ("Lu") Howell, Jr.

The water oak, *Quercus niger*, is the most important wildlife tree of the south. This species has the peculiar habit of allowing its offspring to grow within the shade of the parent tree, creating "uneven aged stands". These stands contain trees of all ages and stages of development. The water oak is also fast becoming a valuable timber species. The tree begins to produce quality acorns at the age of 18 years and will become financially mature for timber at the age of 35 years. That's seventeen years of acorn production from each tree within a given stand. Insist that no more than one third of these trees are removed from a stand during any one cutting of timber, and a sustained yield of timber and mast can be maintained indefinitely. Shady park-like stands such as this one are preferred by turkeys for feeding and loafing. Local folks sometimes call this tree the "pin oak". Find out what species is the number one acorn producer in your area. In my part of the country, this species produces acorns more consistently than any other kind of tree. Fire should be kept out of water oak stands, and in fact, all hardwood stands may be severely damaged by fire. The microorganisms which assist the hardwood stand with the nitrogen cycle are sometimes destroyed by fire and rot causing organisms are introduced through fire wounds on hardwood trees.

Photo from "Roussell Tract" near Jackson, La., on the estate of M. L. Harvey, et al.

This is a typical stand of American beech. Those stands which spring up along steep banked gullies and creeks should be left pretty much intact. The small percentage of land which is lost to more productive timber by leaving these beech stands more than make up for the loss by saving a great deal of topsoil by preventing erosion which follows the foolhardy practices of eliminating these stands with overcutting and poisoning beech trees. There is no sense in losing this turkey habitat and much of the topsoil in the wake of this kind of timber management. Beech stands are productive in terms of producing mast for turkeys during some years. In all years they are a favorite roosting place for turkey flocks. The aesthetic beauty of this type of terrain is unmatched anywhere in the woodlands.

Photo from "Roussell Tract".

Here is a specimen of the cherrybark red oak found in the edge of a woodland tract. The acorns from this tree last a long time and are still good food after much of the other fruit has rotted. I have observed turkeys feeding on red oak acorns in June and July, eating the acorns from the previous fall crop. This particular tree produced 315 pounds of acorns during one year. To fertilize these individual "key trees" is not a bad practice and will enhance the yield of these trees even more. Notice how large the crown is on this edge tree. Much sunlight and water is received by these individuals.

Photo from "Roussell Tract".

The long stretch of edge occupies the eastern most side of a two thousand acre block of hardwood timber. The distance covered in the photograph is more than one half of a mile. The middle of the field in the foreground has been allowed to grow up in low lying dense vegetation. This serves the nesting hens with excellent nesting cover and provides the young newly hatched poults with good escape cover. The edge cover has been well manicured so that turkeys can utilize the area in their search for edge and open site food. Notice the irregularly shaped wood line which provides much surface edge for the turkey flocks. As many as 100 turkeys have been seen in this field.

Photo from "Scott Place" near Jackson, La. Property of James and Leroy Harvey.

Here is a stretch of edge along a grassy opening preferred by turkey flocks. The green in the foreground is bahaia grass; the green in the background is a brown topped millet plot. The millet will be replaced with winter wheat in the fall. The plowed areas have been planted in chufas. This opening has been property fertilized and will provide much food for the turkeys of this area.

Photo from "Turkey Heaven" near Jackson, La., on property of Heidel and Imogene Brown.

This close up of a bahaia grass stand points out the grasshopper, a favored food of young turkeys during the summer months. The numerous seed heads on the bahaia grass stalks also provide abundant food for both young and old turkeys.

Photo from "Turkey Heaven".

The edges receive more sunlight than the deep woods and those mast producing trees found in the edges are likely to produce more mast per tree than those of the deep woods. Careful tending of the desirable mast producers in the edges should be accomplished. A little fertilizer will often increase the productivity of a tree by as much as 100 percent. Woodlots which are elongated or irregularly shaped provide much edge and receive much attention from flocks of turkeys.

Open areas such as pastures and fields are important to the turkeys during the "green" months. During the time of brood raising, summer insects make up an important part of the protein rich diet needed by young growing poults. The grasses of openings produce more insects and larger quantities of grass seeds than the low lying plants of the deep woods. In cultivated fields, the turn rows, ditch banks, and other untillable soil which are allowed to grow up in natural grasses and weeds are good feeding areas for young turkeys. Nutritious foods are found in these places.

Food plots, planted specifically for wildlife, also can provide additional "open space" forage for turkey flocks. These planted food plots should be properly fertilized and kept free of livestock. The long, narrow food plot is better by design than the round or square patch. A variety of crops should be planted in the food plot; winter green crops are mandatory since the plots are primarily intended to supplement the turkey's diet during lean times. Even in years of good mast production on good habitat, the well planned food plot can be a welcomed source of food for turkey flocks. Turkeys should not be disturbed or hunted at all around food plots. Not only is the hunting around food plots unsporting, you can actually condition turkeys to avoid food plots by shooting around these localized feeding areas.

TURKEY FOODS AND FOOD SOURCES

Here is a partial list of some turkey foods and sources. The list certainly is not exhaustive, but will give you an idea of how varied the turkey's diet can and needs to be. Common names of the plants and animals are used.

Tree/Shrubs

Water Oak, Southern Red Oak, Cherrybark Red Oak, Shumard Oak, Nutall Oak, Willow Oak, Black Oak, Overcup Oak, Swamp Chestnut Oak, White Oak, Northern Red Oak, Pin Oak, American Beech, Sweet

Pecan, Hackberry, Flowering Dogwood, Swamp Dogwood, American Elm, Black Cherry, Wild Plum, Black Gum, Tupelo, Sweet Gum, Red Haw, Hornbeam, Winter Huckleberry, Sparkleberry, Summer Huckleberry, Red Mulberry, Magnolia, Yaupon, Red Cedar, French Mulberry, Loblolly Pine, Shortleaf Pine, Spruce Pine

Grasses/Weeds

Bahaia, Dallas grass, Smut grass, Bermuda grass, Coco grass, Johnson grass, Water grass, Curley dock, Common dock, Goat weed, Beggar lice, Greenbrier, Pigweed, Wild barley, Dewberries, Blackberries, Partridge berry, Sunflower, Smart weed

Legumes/Planted Crops

Burr clover, Crimson clover, Dutch clover, Chufas, Corn, Millet, Bicolor lespedeza, Common Vetch, Winter wheat, Rye grass, Cow peas, Brown top millet, Field peas, Peanuts, Soybeans, Hairy Vetch, Fescue, Oats, Subterranean clover, Milo

Animal Foods

Grasshoppers, Leaf hoppers, Crickets, Centipedes, Spiders, Snails, Frogs, Shrimp (prawn), Crawfish, Beetles, Moths, Caterpillars, Salamanders, Ants, Sawyers, Borers, Locusts*

Sometimes we hear the word "cover" used when discussions of habitat are going on. We shall use this term to describe those areas used by turkeys for 1) escape, and 2) nesting. Both nesting and escape cover are ideal if they are located throughout the area of inhabitance by turkey flocks. Hen turkeys should not have to go more than a mile or so in order to find suitable cover for these purposes. An occasional briar patch and dense thicket among the more open terrain is good for the nesting activities of hen turkeys. Nesting success is decidedly better in *low lying thickets* than in the open woods. Old fields which have been allowed to grow up (partially) are good for creating this kind of cover. Small areas which have been extensively cut for timber also provide several years of *low lying dense vegetation* which is ideal escape cover.

I would not recommend a wholesale alteration of the landscape

---

*Some of the above animal and plant foods are listed in a generalized manner. The multitude of species of insect life would be too numerous to list in a writing except in a book by themselves.

just for the purpose of providing this kind of cover. A forty acre clear cut for every six hundred and forty acres of woodland is sufficient.

Younger birds of the year benefit greatly from this kind of cover. They need places like this to escape from predators, especially winged predators. I would prefer to have a small amount of the edge cover made up of this dense vegetation just for that purpose.

Consider the following tips in dealing with your habitat improvements and manipulations:

1. Cultivate the quality mast producing trees within each stand of timber. Find out what species of trees in your part of your country are good mast producers. Don't destroy good stands just for the sake of changing something. Leave the areas turkeys use alone.
2. For optimum yield of mast and timber; establish uneven aged mixed species hardwood stands. Insist that no more than one-third of the trees in a stand be removed during any one cutting of timber.
3. Remove undesirable trees from the close proximity of the more productive trees, but not so many as to remove the canopy from the stand.
4. Keep fire out of hardwood stands.
5. Use controlled burns in pine stands to help establish the desirable understory. Seek knowledgeable assistance in this matter.
6. Construct permanent water sources where they do not exist.
7. Have the soil tested in the open areas, including food plots, so that you can fertilize your "turkey crops" more effectively.
8. Do not allow any timber cutting in those small areas you know to be preferred by turkey flocks for roosting and loafing. Areas along steep banked creeks and ditches and ravines should be left alone in their natural successive state. To leave ten percent of your land alone will save up to fifty percent of the topsoil in some cases.
9. Institute supplemental feeding with good quality grain during winter "hard freezes" or during winter ice storms. The establishment of these feeding areas will condition turkeys to come to that area for hand outs when times are tough. Do no feeding of grain during the summer months at all. This is bad for the nutritional needs of the young poults.
10. Establish bugging areas on untillable soil in agricultural fields.
11. Do no hunting around those areas which have been designed to supplement your flock's need for food and cover.

Predation

Many biologists do not think predators exert a very big limiting force on wild turkey populations. Overall, maybe they don't. In certain places and at certain times, I say that they exert a very pronounced effect on some individual turkey flocks.

It may be true that turkeys will not be exterminated by a bunch of predators other than man. I am not concerned with that. I am occupied with having all the turkeys which can be carried on a given piece of turkey terrain. Predators need to be controlled and their numbers reduced to such a degree until they do not place a significant limiting force on the local populations of wild turkeys.

Nest predation can change nesting success within a given area by more than fifty percent. Nest predation is serious. Many, many species of predators eat birds' eggs of all kinds. Some folks claim that the fertility rate of eggs will be higher by allowing skunks, dogs, raccoons, crows, and other predators to destroy nests. They say that nest predators will rob those nests containing rotten eggs and thereby actually help the turkey population. Baloney! A rotten egg isn't going to hatch out anyway and anyone who believes that nest predation is limited to only those nests containing rotten eggs does not know much about the predators themselves. I have observed many nests which have been destroyed by nest robbers where I have not been able to find any evidence at all to indicate there was a rotten egg aboard.

Most nest pilfering is a random sort of event. Nest predators just happen up on the nest and feast on the eggs, rotten ones and vital ones alike. The random approach to finding turkey nests by predators is typical of most species except the crow. More about the crow later.

Most small children at those little functions called "Easter Egg Hunts" just run around like a bunch of chickens with their heads cut off. Some enterprising kids are more systematic in their search for the eggs, but most do just scamper around looking for eggs where ever they happen to wander. If you had one hundred little kids at a typical egg hunt and had only fifty at another egg hunt, it would take much longer for the fewer numbered group of kids to find the same number of hidden eggs.

The same would be true for turkey nest predators. If you reduce the predator population by fifty percent or more, then it would take the surviving predators much longer to destroy the same number of nests. Perhaps it would even take enough time (more than the length of the nesting period) to allow some nests to hatch out which would probably have been robbed if twice the number of nest robbers were out and about. If a nest had a smelly egg in it, it would not take long for even a very small number of predators to find that particular nest.

Of course, there are a few predators which search deligently for eggs. These types will find more than those predators which just ramble around, stumbling upon a few nests. In open areas, the crow is a very thorough searcher for turkey nests. Turkeys which nest in the open woods often lose their eggs to these bandits.

The crow is a good reason to have that low lying dense thicket within some areas of the habitat to enhance nesting success for turkey hens. Crows do not search well in thickets like they do in the open woods.

A pair of crows will alight near a solitary hen out of her nest for a short break. The pair of crows will be silent and very stealthy. They will employ a leap frog method of following the hen back to her nest in a fashion similar to one finding a bee tree. If the nesting hen is not watchful and careful, she will lose her entire clutch of eggs to these villians. Sometimes, the crows will badger a nesting hen for days and once they discover the time of day the hen gets off her nest, they become extremely persistent in finding the nest.

Feral dogs and coyotes with their keen noses are also effective nest predators. They also are very effective killers of little poults still in the downy stage and not yet able to fly away from the four legged predators. The canine type of predator has the intelligence to become practiced at what he does. Here are some accounts of how the coyote works.

A place we call "the tree house pasture" always has several groups of young broods around it during the bugging times of the year. In the early summer of 1983, I was observing an old bearded hen with fourteen little downy poults in the open area. Suddenly a coyote dashed into the field and was in the midst of the feeding turkeys before you could blink. Of course, the little ones scattered and became still. The 'yote began a careful search for the little turkeys, ignoring the frustrated old hen. He found a little turkey and ran into the woods with it. While the old hen was still walking around in circles, the coyote returned and found another young poult. I then intervened hy hollering at the coyote. He left.

The very next day, the same bearded hen was in another grassy opening with her surviving babies. This field was about one fourth of a mile from the tree house pasture. The 'yote appeared again and repeated the performance of the day before. I got a clear shot at the coyote two days later as he rushed the brood in yet another field. I eliminated the coyote. The old hen's fine brood had been reduced to nine little ones by then. After I shot the coyote, the hen lost only one more of her young ones; to what, I do not know. She raised eight fine youngsters, but I am convinced that the coyote would have reduced her productivity to zero if I had not come along with my rifle.

Another time, my sister-in-law was observing an old hen with sixteen young ones in the pasture behind her house every evening. One afternoon, a coyote made that typical dash into the turkey group. The hen dutifully went into her crippled act and was surprised when the coyote made a lightning quick lunge at her. The predator ate the hen on the spot. No one knew what became of the poults because the little ones were never seen again.

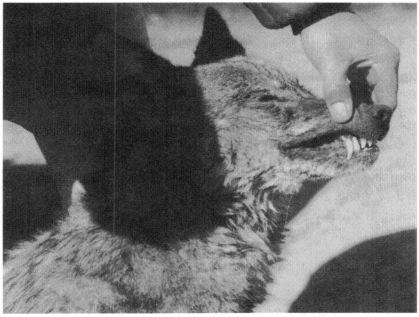

"The only good coyote . . ."

You cannot convince me that predators are insignificant within the dynamics of a turkey flock population.

Some studies have indicated that buffer animals work in the favor of game populations. A buffer animal is an animal which serves as prey for predators in the place of game animals. The theory is that if you have enough buffer animals, like rats and mice, then predators won't bother the game animals very much. This might work to a degree, but large numbers of buffer animals lead to a large number of predators also. Then those random encounters between turkeys and predators will likely increase. My idea of the best policy involves thinning out the predators and then the buffer animals will feed the surviving predators very nicely.

Trapping, when and where it is legal, is one of the best ways to control the predator populations within a given locale. Like all outdoor activities, trapping needs to be closely monitored and common sense must be used where the presence of domestic pets may shed a negative light on the activity. Only responsible personnel should be allowed to trap and the setting and checking of traps should be regular. All efforts to make this endeavor of trapping with steel jawed traps as humane as possible should be undertaken. Of course, the income from trapping can turn out to be a welcomed benefit to some folks.

In terms of predator control by trapping and shooting, there are only a few species which should be pursued for the purpose of helping the wild turkey populations. While a species like the Red Tailed Hawk may occasionally feed on young turkeys when the opportunity affords itself, do not waste your time doing more harm than good by pursuing these minor offenders. What follows is a partial list of the common predators of wild turkeys at each successive stage of the birds' development. Begin to think of how we might assist turkeys and not become engaged in an all out war on all predators native to our land.

Egg-Nest predators: Striped skunk, Spotted skunk, Common crow, Wood rat, Cotton rat, Norway rat, Opposum, Feral dog, Coyote, Gray fox, Red fox, Weasel, Mink, Raccoon

Downy Poult predators: Common crow, Feral dog, Coyote, Horned owl, Bobcat, Sharp shinned hawk

Juvenile/Poult predators: Horned owl, Bobcat

Adult Turkey predators: Horned owl, Bobcat

As you see, the list of effective predators becomes smaller with each successive stage of developing turkeys. In fact, there are only a few species of predators which I will call "impact species", which are strongly detrimental to turkey flocks in localized areas. The impact species list follows. Probably more strenuous control measures should be undertaken towards controlling the numbers of these predators. They are listed in order of impact.

Impact species: 1) feral dog, 2) coyote, 3) raccoon, 4) common crow, 5) Striped skunk, 6)Horned owl, 7) bobcat.

These species do not make up an exhaustive list of predators which may effect local populations, but I believe they are the most serious offenders, at least in the part of the country where I live and hunt. These characters eat up plenty of our recreational opportunities. Of course no woodland would be complete without the presence of some bobcats; keep that in mind as you attempt to help your game species flourish.

Weather

It has often been stated that we can do nothing about the weather. At times there are very poor reproduction years within a flock of turkeys simply because the weather was poor. This has been true for a long time and will probably continue to be true since we cannot do anything about the weather.

Cold rainy weather during the hatching period destroys a lot of young broods. Floods obviously wash some nests away from time to time. The main problem, however, arises when the little newly hatched poults still in the downy stage get soaking wet repeatedly. They are not properly insulated at this stage of their development and the brood hen must cover them and warm them with her own body heat. At this stage of the young ones' development, the birds also have an incredibly high rate of metabolism and burn up energy at an extremely high rate. These factors, if the little ones continue to get wet and require brooding, and have to go without regularly feeding, cause their resistance to drop to zero. They get pneumonia types of diseases and die very easily and quickly. The phenomenon destroys many, many young turkeys during wet and cool hatching seasons.

The most critical period occurs during the time of the spring when the majority of hens are scheduled to hatch. While the turkey hen is extremely persistent at re-nesting, that first clutch is the largest and the long growing season ahead of that time quite naturally tends to produce larger numbers of juvenile turkeys when late summer and early fall approaches. Turkey hens which attempt second and third nestings do have some success, but the first wave of hatchings produce those bumper crops of turkeys in those banner years.

To combat these losses to weather, we must reduce the other limiting factors so that when poor hatching and raising success comes as a result of the weather, the losses won't be so devastating.

Disease

Of all the limiting factors, I fear disease more than the others. Other than the common diseases, which in themselves reach bad proportions at times, I worry about some new exotic poultry disease. A new disease is always the most deadly on any kind of population. I fear, that sooner or later, somehow, a strange new disease is going to be accidentally introduced into our wild flocks. I know what the results will be—Devastating!

The tried and true habit of keeping domestic poultry off the turkey range will help prevent this kind of catastrophe. Every once in a while, I hear about some folks turning birds loose which have been hatched in captivity. In many parts of farming country, people occasionally uncover nests during their pasture clipping activities, then take the eggs home and hatch them out under some kind of domestic poultry stock. Some of these birds are returned to the wild by well-meaning enthusiastic do-gooders. I know of a farmer near Brookhaven, Mississippi who has turned at least fifty of these birds loose. Of course, few of these kinds of turkeys survive more than a few hours or days in the wild. The problem will come when these returned birds live long enough to infect the native wild populations with a wide ranging, fast spreading disease.

I would not use barnyard fertilizer on my food plots for anything and it might be a good idea to have wildlife biologists check your kills during the open season for any signs of infection or disease or parasites. Lack-luster appearing turkeys and very light weighted turkeys should be examined every time.

At the first sign of sickness among your turkey flocks, you should contact the very top of the Game Department in your state. Take no chances. In the case of wildlife diseases, an ounce of prevention is worth a ton of cure.

We could continue this little chapter into a book in itself. Maybe we will one day—but I hope I have given you some food for thought on the subject of helping our cause. If you are really serious about making your turkey hunting better, hire a hard working biologist to assist you. It will well be worth the effort. Consider the following checklist of priorities in dealing with managing the wild turkey.

MANAGEMENT CHECKLIST/PRIORITIES
1. Clamp down on illegal hunting activities by assisting law enforcement agencies.
2. Restrict your own harvest on a given area.
3. Improve and cultivate your natural habitat.
4. Supplement food and water sources on the habitat.
5. Control impact predators.
6. Exercise caution concerning exposure of wild turkeys to disease.
7. Pray for good brood hatching weather.
8. Cultivate private landowner interests in wild game species.

14 Please Be Careful, the Woods Are Full of Hunters

Straight down the log road from the clearing, a big gobbler was just absolutely tearing it up. I eased up to the edge of the clearing and right away noticed the dusting holes all around the place. What a good setup; and very quickly and as quietly as possible, I got properly hidden with a good view of the whole little clearing which was only about twenty-five yards wide.

After making a series of calls and getting a quick double gobble from the turkey, I leaned back on a tree and began what was to be a good thirty minute wait. I sure was feeling good about my lucky fortunes and the fact that I didn't get into the area until well after sunup didn't seem to matter anymore.

At last I could see the old tom coming down the log road following a pair of hens. Where the road ran into the clearing was a clump of thick bushes; I guess the shrubs were thirty to thirty-five yards away. Slowly the turkeys came on. Again I mentally calculated the distance to the edge of the clearing and decided that my little single barreled twenty gauge would kill the gobbler anywhere in the clearing, but not one step beyond. I mentally prepared myself to let the gobbler be completely in the clearing and standing tall before I shot.

As expected, the gobbler made a long pause just outside the clearing and let the hens parade right on out in the open. I was already following him with the bead when a tiny movement in the bushes caught my eye and the gobbler's eye too. Up went the long neck as the gobbler became erect and still as the ground he was standng on. I could not believe how long that turkey's neck was. He was only thirty-eight steps away, and I remember wishing for a twelve gauge as the tom stayed put for an eternity; by now the hens had their heads up too and were purring a little. Suddenly there was a rustling inside the bushes and the gobbler was instantly somewhere else. The hens ran too.

Out of the bushes stepped a hunter; he was camouflaged from head to toe and even had pine needle clusters stuck in his cap. My goodness, I could have shot him if I had risked a long shot at the turkey because the hunter had been hidden directly in line between me and the bird. All I could see was the head and stretched out neck of the gobbler and if I had been loaded with four's in a three inch magnum twelve gauge, I might have taken my shot when I had the chance.

I whistled, stood up, and walked over to the hunter who was yawning and stretching. His first comment was something about the area being all hunted out with nothing left around but a few nesting hens. I was a little bit amused at this point, but I can assure you that no laughing matter would have been at hand had I taken a shot. The incident shook me up the more I realized what a terrible accident could have taken place.

I learned that the hunter's vehicle was parked about a mile to the north and mine was some four hundred yards to the south. The hunter informed me that he had been hiding in those bushes since long before daylight and was asleep (apparently) when I sneaked up to the clearing late in the morning.

Turkey season accounts for more hunting accidents each year than most of the other seasons combined—This is really startling since the numbers of turkey hunters, although increasing rapidly, do not come close to being what they are for some of the other types of hunting. Every year a growing number of people are killed, blinded, or maimed by turkey hunters, who, for one reason or another shoot other hunters. I know the nature of all this hiding and sounding like a turkey makes us highly vulnerable to getting shot, but there must be some things we can do to cut down on these tragedies.

Most turkey hunting accidents which occur fall into one of three different categories. Below are listed the three categories along with some tips and/or rules with suggestions to help you have a more safe hunting experience.

Category 1. Basic Gun Safety

Some hunters allow their guns to discharge and injure themselves or someone else due to improper handling of a loaded weapon. Most of these accidents can be eliminated by following simple basic rules of gun safety. Responsible people are knowledgeable to these basic rules, but we will list them again.

a. Unload your gun before climbing fences and negotiating places where the footing may be tricky.
b. Check your safety apparatus frequently.
c. Unload your gun before getting into a vehicle.
d. Never travel on an ATV with a loaded weapon.
e. Do not lean your gun against trees.
f. Be extra careful with your weapon after you make a kill.
g. Always double check your gun before entering a building.
h. Consider a gun to be loaded and handle it accordingly whether you believe it to be loaded or not.
i. Do not point a gun in the direction of another person.

Of course you could add to this list: The bottom line with these types of accidents is that you must realize the gun you hunt turkeys with is a very dangerous weapon which will snuff out human life if care is not taken.

Category 2. Shooting at a turkey and hitting another hunter.

This type of accident occurs when one hunter shoots someone he was not aware of, or when two people hunting together lose track of where they are in relation to each other. Bad judgement on the part of overly excited hunters account for some of these shootings. Consider the following:

a. When hunting with a partner, hunt side by side or hunt a very long distance apart.
b. Don't hunt with large sized shot.
c. Don't shoot a rifle, even where they are legal.
d. Don't use decoys, you are asking for trouble.
e. Don't sneak up on a gobbling bird.
f. Don't attempt to set up on a gobbler which you know is being worked by another hunter.
g. IF YOU ARE HUNTING ON PRIVATE LAND, MAKE SURE YOU ARE WHERE YOU ARE SUPPOSED TO BE. TRESPASSING GETS A CONSIDERABLE NUMBER OF PEOPLE SHOT EACH YEAR. (ACCIDENTLY)

Category 3. Shooting another hunter which has been mistaken for a turkey

This category seems almost too ridiculous to talk about. How in the world can people be so stupid? To shoot a hunter for a turkey is just about as irresponsible as you can get. While some people do sound very much like wild turkeys and the noises associated with hunting may be similar to a turkey moving around, I have never seen a human being which remotely looked like a big old gobbler with a long swinging beard.

I have heard of people being so excited until vague objects in the woods became real objects to them. I have often been looking into a stretch of heavy cover myself and imagined that I could see a big buck or gobbler, but not once have I ever considered shooting at such an object. When I shoot, I want to kill something—and that something is the game which I am pursuing at the time. Man, you can't consistently kill wild gobblers unless you do it right. In order to be successful, the bird has to be standing before you. Now what excuse would anyone have for taking any kind of shot other than the ones I describe in the chapter "Stealth"? None whatsoever.

Still, we have to be concerned about those "crazies" which will make their way into the turkey woods. Here are some tips on preserving your own hide.

a. Do not wear colors which suggest turkeys or other game. Especially do not wear red or white.
b. If you think or suspect other hunters may be in the area, don't use gobbler imitations.
c. Sit with your back to a large tree.
d. Avoid sneaking up on gobbling turkeys.
e. Alert approaching hunters to your presence before they get in range to do you damage if they are surprised.
f. If a pickup or other vehicle is in your area, go somewhere else.
g. Speak in a clearly human voice to hunters which do manage to sneak up close to you—leave no doubt that you are human.

Some other thoughts concerning turkey hunting accidents. First of all, we could crack down on trespassers and poachers. That group of outlaws accounts for a large percentage of shooting accidents. This is simply because they are in turkey woods where, by the nature of their activity, no one knows where they are and often they don't know where other hunters are either. Poachers and trespassers run a very high risk of shooting other hunters or being shot themselves.

The poacher argues that there isn't enough land to go around for all hunters and justifies his enfringement on other folks' private lands. It's a shame that there are more people than there are wild turkeys, but that is a fact.

Our little hunting fraternity in Jackson, La., bagged twenty-eight gobblers last season and we had twenty-four different people hunting at one time or another. We are sorry we could not accommodate any more people than that, but it would have placed more pressure on the game than would have been good management if we had allowed any more hunters to participate. And the margin of safety we allowed for each hunter on each day of hunting was what we felt was necessary. Everyone who hunts with us has a specific area to hunt, and other hunters are not allowed in the close proximity to where a person is scheduled to hunt. We have never had an accident, thank God, and we don't intend to if we can help it. As I have stated quite emphatically, It's a One Man Game, to hunt turkeys otherwise is dangerous and less than what it is best designed to be in terms of recreational enjoyment. It is better to have one day alone in the woods with the birds and the elements than it is to have two weeks in the woods with a crowd of other folks trying to do the same thing you are attempting.

And the poacher, just because he is not as fortunate or as industrious as some of us, does not have the right to endanger the lives of all the other people out in the woods. All over the country, the problem of overcrowed hunting conditions exist and are likely to remain so.

The private leases we hunt on are the safest places to be. The illegal hunter is about the only one who will do you any harm.

But what do we do about all of us who hunt the lands which are open to the public? It is not feasible to monitor the turkey hunts so closely as we do on private lands. There are sometimes more people out there after gobblers than there are gobblers.

The various state agencies responsible for setting seasons and bag limits could do a great deal to ease the pressure situations. I am in favor of having at least a month of open season and am also in favor of reducing the bag limit of gobblers to only one bird per season. And I know a lot of shooting incidents and deaths would be avoided by making only *long-bearded* gobblers legal.

Some states set ridiculously short seasons and give their hunting public an unreasonably short period of time to get their birds. Why, I might even be a little nervous myself, even though I have been responsible for the death of over three hundred gobblers in four states during my hunting life. Imagine, those of you who do not hunt these short season states, how much pressure would be placed upon the hunter who is told he must kill a gobbler before the coming weekend.

It is a pretty sound bet that most legal hunting of a trophy animal, like a wild gobbler, is a nerve wracking experience to most normal human beings who are enthralled by the natural experiences involved in pursuing wild gobblers. I say that the accident rate would decrease if the average hunter were convinced that he had to see a long swinging beard hanging from a bird before he fired his shot. It would also be reasonable to assume that a longer season would make the average hunter less anxious to shoot something, to shoot anything, in such a big hurry as to make a critical mistake.

If the legal limit were reduced, there would be fewer hunters in the woods on a given day. I mean, a large percentage of the hunters who got their bird would be gone from the woods soon thereafter. Of course, some folks, like myself, would probably continue to take other people hunting and try to call up gobblers for them. But there would still be far fewer guns out and about. The fewer shots we have to take, by fewer guns, the fewer hunters will be accidently shot. Fewer guns, fewer shots,—fewer shot.

You may have already got my message about the small gauge gun and its limited range and killing power. I have killed many big birds with the big guns and the copper coated four's, but nowadays I have gone back to where I came from. I hunt with a small gun loaded with small shot just like I did when I was a youngster. I don't (can't) take long shots, it's more sporting, and I am much less likely to kill some human being sitting out there hidden from me and the turkeys.

Until other changes and the ones I suggest are made, let's please be careful. The shooting of a bird is not worth accidently shooting one of our fellow human beings.

Have a good time!

Sonny Palmer

15 The Turkey Hunting Fraternity

Whether real or imagined, I will go from here believing that real bona fide turkey hunters are of a calibre which is a considerable cut above the other types of hunting groups. Unlike the deer hunting groups, where back-biting and jealousy seem to reign supreme, the turkey hunting fraternity pulls together and each individual within the group prays for the good luck of the fellow participants within his little circle.

The nature of turkey hunting in its purest form of sport, calling the long-bearded birds in the spring, lends itself to bringing out the best in hunters and people. Other forms of hunting fail to accomplish this except on the rarest of occasions. The realization that this game is indeed a sport of one on one competition with the single bird of a species designed for entertainment, tends to create friendship bonds which endure for lifetimes among fellow hunters.

It is the only sport where there is genuine pleasure taken from the escape of a quarry which we desire to be dead so strongly. Every spring we look forward to, not only slaying a long-beard or two, but to the company of our companions who howl with real joy at the antics of the hunter and prey alike. Every man hopes that some of the game escapes, and yes, we wish to put a gobbler or two to rest also.

It has been my good fortune to have been associated with some real outstanding hunters and people during my tenure as a card carrying turkey hunter. The present group with whom I am associated are among the finest folks on earth, and any spring would be a blank without their company. Here are some sage comments about turkey hunting from the regular members of our little group.

Bobby Joe King shows off a handsome gobbler taken on our private lease in West Feliciana Parish. Says B.J., "The gobblers of a particular ridge system on our lease tend to circle when they are approaching a caller. I killed this bird by first getting him to answer me and then I moved to another spot a hundred yards east of where I called from. Sure enough, in a short while the gobbler circled around my original hiding place and came within range of me. I shot him at a distance of twenty yards." B.J. is an advocate of moving around until he feels like he is in the perfect place to collect a gobbling turkey. He has a very high percentage of kills per days of hunting. Maybe we are lucky that his engineering profession keeps him too busy to hunt as often as the rest of us.

Bob Price is our resident farmer. Bob reports, "A dependable source of food is necessary to hold any kind of game. The wild turkey is no exception. I get as much pleasure from raising wild animals as I do from harvesting them. Having grown up during the depression years, when there were no wild turkeys to be found, has made me appreciate the bountiful supply of game we have in our fields and forests now." Bob also offers the advice of not wearing a headnet if you happen to wear glasses as he does. "Headnets cause condensation to occur on eye glasses, and that can be a serious hindrance to a hunter trying to see a gobbler in a thickly forested area."

Van Morgan bagged this fine specimen on a frosty spring morning. Van prefers deep woods hunting and strongly believes that most spooked turkeys are created by human noises. "Quiet feet are absolutely a must when getting into a position to see any game; the wild turkey requires extreme quietness on the part of the hunter. Snugly fitting boots and shoes are the most important part of your equipment. A simple shot can be had with any shotgun, but noisy foot gear will prevent the best shotgun from bringing down very many gobblers." Van also insists that gobbling birds are more fun to fool with in the deep woods, claiming that deep woods birds feel more secure and will gobble more freely than those on the edges.

Butch Trahan is one of the best woodsmen to be found anywhere. Being a muzzle-loader enthusiast, Butch gave this old gobbler a try with his double barrel percussion shotgun and was successful in bagging the bird with a load of #nine shot. "Don't fool with a big gobbler in the afternoon. If you know where a big bird is roosting, try him during the first couple of hours of daylight and then leave him alone the rest of the day. Undisturbed gobblers will continue their routine and eventually you will get lucky." Butch spends much of every turkey season hunting and calling with his father-in-law, Sonny Palmer. Sonny has missed exactly one gobbler in all of his years of hunting. He is a deadly shot because he does not shoot until everything is just right.

Tom Woodside, Jr. (left), is our senior game warden in this district and does not get to hunt as often as he would like. The efforts of Tom keep the people of the Feliciana Parishes well supplied with native game and we appreciate what he does. "I would rather bag one gobbler than ten buck deer," indicates what kind of person Tom is. Tom uses a wingbone type of caller and a Turpin yelper. Tom feels like the most common error hunters make when hunting turkeys is to call too much. Close behind the too much calling habit, is the fact that the average hunter does not have any idea where the turkeys are when he goes after them. Prehand scouting is important and generally speaking, it takes three or four days to get a nice gobbler.

Mark Abernathy, (right) has killed a lot of gobblers. He takes time off to hunt and bagged this gobbler on his homeplace near Centreville, Mississippi. Mark's strong suit is patience. I have known him to sit patiently for three or more hours if he believes gobblers are in the area. Mark is also a stickler for details and does not leave a stone unturned when it comes to getting prepared for going turkey hunting. "When I get ready to go turkey hunting, I get mentally ready and then I block out all other things from my mind. If I decide that I must wait at some junction of woods roads all day, then I go do that all day. If it becomes necessary to get down into some branch head and duel the gobbler with my caller, then I stick to that game plan. I don't plan on letting some gobbler mess up my plans."

The Missouri trio visits us every spring and stays about a week to hunt our gobblers. We have a fine time and usually they go back to Missouri with some good trophies like these and they always go back with some wild tales to spread, I'm sure.

Joe Bowman (left) is a very persistent hunter and one of the most knowledgeable outdoorsmen around. "Turkey hunting is among my favorite hunting activities — and I have many. I find the birds of the south to be very similar in nature to the gobblers in Missouri, although these Louisiana toms may be a little bit more spooky and may not gobble quite as much. In all areas that I have hunted, learning the areas to be hunted seem prerequisite to having a good chance to get a gobbler. Late morning gobblers respond to calls well in both Louisiana and Missouri."

Dick Curnow (middle) is the comedian of our group. His jokes and good sense of humor keeps us all in stitches. Dick is also a very serious turkey hunter. "The cluck and variations of it have been my favorite call; in fact, the majority of the birds I have called have responded to my cluck imitations." Dick is also a Model 12 collector and really appreciates fine weapons. One or more of his sons accompany him each spring on his turkey hunting escapades and a good time is had by all. We residents especially get a real kick out of it when one of Dick's young sons manages to outdo the old man. Joe and Dick get a thrill from those occasions too.

Matthew Curnow (right) bagged his gobbler after watching him from a distance on two successive mornings. Matt is developing into a fine hunter with the sense of pride found in the rest of us. We need more kids like Matt.

William Yarbrough is known as "the gadget man" to many youngsters and hunters from this area. If there is a gadget on the market with a practical use in the turkey woods, William owns one of them—and he uses them too. William's use of a topographical map has been developed into a fine art and this tool has become a valuable part of William's accouterment. William's real strength as a hunter is centered around the extra sense of his to pick out the correct place to hunt wild gobblers. He can properly identify "a turkey place" when he sees it and nine times out of ten will find a nice gobbler or two there. He is one of the most diligent searchers for game of anyone I know and sometimes will walk ten miles in a day just to see a little fresh scratching. Of all the hunters within our area, William has allowed more gobblers to walk away than anyone I know of. This attests to his high value of the wild turkey. He is the backbone of our little turkey hunting group.

"Lu" and Jody

"LU" HOWELL

His double barreled Parker had a peculiar ringing report which signaled the death toll for many a long-bearded gobbler. For a large man, he was unbelievably quiet on his feet, had a keen eye, could hear a turkey drumming farther than me, and was a deadly shot. He was a total hunter and was the one man on earth who made me actually feel sorry for the gobblers he pursued.

You see, the late J. T. ("Lu") Howell, Jr. bagged hundreds, yes, hundreds, of trophy gobblers. In fact, of the vast experience and know-how possessed by "Lu", a small percentage of it was transferred to me. At least one-half of the turkey hunting lore found in this writing was pointed out to the hunter by none other than "Lu" Howell.

During my training exercises with "Lu", it was a persistence at doing things his way in the woods which made me a better hunter. For example, I would have never dreamed of not calling a gobbler I could actually see. "Lu" always insisted that a gobbler which had strolled into view should not be called further. I am still amazed at how the birds will come closer, quicker, with no additional coaxing after they are in sight.

"Lu"'s tactic of climbing trees to spy on turkey toms from afar is a classic maneuver for getting into position on turkeys out in this rolling farm country.

I'll never forget the morning we marched in the opposite direction of a violently gobbling bird. I was very objectionable to this move, but "Lu" had promised the turkey would respond better if we placed ourselves a long ways from the roost tree. That particular gobbler zig-zagged over a quarter of a mile to our hiding place; whereupon, "Lu" blew him away with that gun of his.

Man, I could write a whole book on "Lu" Howell hunting stories—maybe I will one day. Here's a story you might like.

"Lu" called one night and announced that he knew exactly where a couple of big gobblers were roosting. "We need to make a raid," he reported. A storm was brewing, but "Lu" was a hard man to say no to. We left the house the next morning just after the storm passed and some forty-five minutes before daylight. "Lu" turned down a little gravel road and soon shut the truck lights off. I made some comments about not being able to see, and "Lu" retorted about my lack of a sense of adventure. Anyway, "Lu" claimed to know every foot of the gravel road and was worried that the lights would spook the turkeys way off down in the woods. We continued down the road in the pitch black darkness until suddenly we were half upside down, hanging precariously on the edge of a ten foot deep hole. The storm had completely washed away a little bridge and we were in a helluva fix. When I rolled the window down, the raging torrent of flood water could be heard from just under the front axle of "Lu"'s pickup. I also had the sensation of being on some sort of see-saw. "Dammit!", shouted "Lu" and with that he bailed out of the truck with some last second instructions to keep the truck in reverse while he pushed us out. Now the water was up to "Lu"'s ears, but so help me, the man pushed the three-quarter ton pickup out of that creek.

While "Lu" was wringing out his clothes and drying his head with *my* shirt, I made the comment about him using leverage rather than strength to get the truck out. Whereupon he threatened to drive the truck back into the hole just to see if I could push it out like he did. I declined to try.

"Lu" climbed back into the truck and with much backing up and turning around, turned on the lights and blew the horn a number of long loud blasts. "What's all that for?", I asked. "Since you ain't got the nerve to swim that creek, I figure we had better go somewhere else. I want to spook these turkeys real good so they won't gobble at all this morning while we are hunting somewhere else," explained "Lu".

When we got to our second hunting place, it was very late for a turkey hunt. The wetness was just off the grass as we approached a big field where a creek ran along one side. I could tell that the woods were turkeyish down there even though this way my first trip on the property we were hunting.

As we stepped into the field, a couple of hens spotted us and ran like hell to the north and into five square miles of big woods. "Lu" knocked me to the ground and we crawled into a ditch at the edge of the field. As luck would have it, as we were sitting in the ditch wondering, "what next?", one of the biggest long-bearded gobblers I ever saw came strolling into the field. His beard was as thick as a man's arm and he had that walking swagger to him that told all about his importance in the scheme of things in those parts. "Cut-tabba-tabba-tabba-wump-wump", he announced his arrival. "Cut! Cut! kuk-kuk-kuk-kuk", I replied. The old bird stretched, thought, and strutted out there in the field three hundred yards away. "Lu" instructed me to put my head behind the ditch bank and gobble at the bird. I did, and the turkey gobbled and strutted some more. I did no more calling until three other gobblers showed up to join the Sultan. The new arrivals did not have their heads lit up like the old turkey and acted a bit submissive to the main turkey. All four gobblers finally adjusted their wings and began a long steady march towards "Lu" and me. When they went down into a little dip in the field, "Lu" leaned up on the right side of a small pine growing out of the ditch and I propped myself up on the left side.

Twice the old one stopped to strut while the others waited a few feet ahead. When the three were finally at thirty-five yards and the old one was strutting at forty-five yards, I felt the Parker on my right begin to inch upwards. Very slowly I put my hand on the gun and whispered, "Wait, let them get closer and we'll get two of 'em". "Lu" relaxed and the big gun sank back to its resting position. When the old one stepped inside of thirty-five yards, I snapped up my shotgun and put his lights out. I won't repeat what "Lu" had to say after he had zapped one of the other gobblers.

All is fair though, "Lu" killed the next two while we were hunting together. I was finally allowed to shoot again some three weeks later and after all the smoke had cleared, was surprised to find that "Lu" had shot also. We must have shot at exactly the same instant, because I did not hear "Lu" shoot and he did not hear me fire either. We both offered our spent shells for evidence and an examination of the dead gobbler revealed both sixes (mine) and fours ("Lu"'s) in the neck of the turkey.

I had forgotten my carrying rope and tied the turkey up with "Lu's" rope and was proudly carrying the gobbler across a coco grass field when the rope came untied like it had been cut with a knife. The knot on the end of the rope hit me in the eye and I couldn't see out of that eye for several days. I did recover to hunt some more with my friend "Lu".

We may never fully recover from "Lu"'s untimely death as a result of malignant tumors. The big fellow was the best friend of many folks, including me.

Maybe all is not lost. I see a lot of "Lu" Howell in his son Jody. "Lu" instilled within Jody a great many of those values upon which we all cling. Within the context of this writing, young Jody Howell has been taught by his father and his grandfathers to conserve and preserve those things of nature—including the wild turkey. Many of Jody's other relatives share this attitude and many of "Lu" 's friends hold a common bond through outdoor activities.

Gee, on those crisp spring mornings when the woods are rattling with gobbler talk, I'll always think of "Lu". It will be a great consolation if men all across this country are teaching their youngsters those same conservation principles. Let the turkey hunting fraternity be vital forever.

Made in the USA
Columbia, SC
29 June 2022